YOU'RE STILL THAT GIRL

you're still
THAT GIRL

Get Over Your Abusive
Ex for Good!

SUZANNA QUINTANA

NEW YORK

LONDON • NASHVILLE • MELBOURNE • VANCOUVER

You're Still That Girl

Get Over Your Abusive Ex for Good!

Published in New York, New York, by Morgan James Publishing in partnership with Difference Press. Morgan James is a trademark of Morgan James, LLC.
www.MorganJamesPublishing.com

ISBN 9781642796681 paperback
ISBN 9781642796698 eBook
ISBN 9781642796704 audiobook
Library of Congress Control Number: 2019943961

Cover Design by:
Megan Dillon
megan@creativeninjadesigns.com

Interior Design by:
Christopher Kirk
www.GFSstudio.com

Morgan James is a proud partner of Habitat for Humanity Peninsula and Greater Williamsburg. Partners in building since 2006.

Get involved today! Visit
MorganJamesPublishing.com/giving-back

For all those women who raised their voices and shared their stories so that I could find my way out of the darkness and into the light, thank you. This book is dedicated to you.

TABLE OF CONTENTS

YOU ARE NOT ALONE

"Silence is the most powerful scream."
– Anonymous

Y ou chose this book for a reason. More than curiosity, something compelled you to open it up to this first page. You're hurting and you haven't been able to explain it – not to friends, not to family – because you don't even understand it yourself. After all, you're not in the relationship that was killing you any longer, right? So why is it you can't just move on? Why is it so hard to put the past behind you? Maybe you've even begun to feel a bit crazy or like there is something wrong with you. People in your past told you that you were too emotional and too sensitive; so, what if they were right? What if you've convinced yourself that it is all in your head and that somehow, in some way, the fact that you can't move forward (or if you do it's followed by ten steps back) is actually all your fault? On some days you might feel sick, as if your pain has manifested physically. You find yourself staring out windows, searching for hope but feeling void of any. And on those particularly grueling days, you believe your life will never get better and that this is as good as it will ever get.

There is a reason you chose this book.

Now take a deep breath, because you're not alone anymore.

I see you. I've been you. I've lived in that same darkness, on the verge of surrender to life as I knew it, believing it would never get any better and I deserved all the pain I was suffocating from.

And I'm here to tell you something. I'm here to tell you the truth, and the truth is that *it does get better*. You can move on past heartbreak and enjoy a life of peace and happiness and love that you've always dreamed about. In fact, a life that you deserve. This darkness you exist in now is lying to you. Those voices in your head that tell you you're crazy or weak or need to grow a thicker skin are not yours. They're imposters masquerading as someone you used to trust and love and would even have died for.

The light is trying to get in – right now as you read these words on the page – but you can't yet feel its warmth because you're trapped in an illusion that only benefits the one who broke your heart. Maybe you left recently or even months ago, or you were discarded by someone you loved with all your heart and the pain refuses to go away. Maybe you even went back once (or more) but then reached your breaking point and decided to never return, though you can't make sense of why it hurts so bad. Maybe you've been out of the relationship for more than a year but you're still feeling the aftereffects: you're still emotionally attached and unable to move on because of this attachment. Or maybe you think that you've moved on but now you're involved in another relationship that is causing you a similar pain.

This is the illusion that prevents you from stepping fully into the light that is patiently waiting for you and has a space reserved with your name on it. Here in this space, your unconditional honesty and raw vulnerability are required. But to claim it, you must be willing to travel into those dark places that before you've desperately tried to avoid. Then you need to make good friends, best friends, with the one who holds the key to the door of your journey ahead. She already knows of your suffering, and she also knows the way forward, if only you'd take her hand.

But first: Wherever you are in this moment, take a deep breath. Seriously, *you need to breathe*. I don't care who's around you right now or what chaos you've left behind or are about to head into. You need a long, deep breath.

I'm not kidding. I'll wait.

And exhale.

You know that girl I'm talking about. The one from your past. The one who had Wonder Woman–sized courage and couldn't be swayed, bought, or bullied into submission whether she was five or nine or fourteen – that girl whose spirit had yet to be trampled, whose instincts had yet to be dulled, whose compassion had yet to be exploited. That girl played and ran and competed right along with the boys in the neighborhood, having yet to be told that she wasn't good enough, strong enough, or worthy enough because of her "girl-ness." That girl's dreams couldn't even fit into the Grand Canyon because of their scope and size; she wrote secrets in her diary, had more imaginary friends than real ones, and talked to her stuffed animals and also to the moon at night before drifting off to sleep. That girl knew without a doubt who she was, what she was capable of, and what she deserved even if all other outside forces – mother, father, sibling, grandparent, friend – were trying to convince her otherwise.

Yes, *that* girl.

And yet in all her wisdom and glorious ways, what she didn't know was the power of *time*. She didn't know that the years would wear her down, making her unable to bear the onslaught of the people she loved the most being the very ones who would betray her and send her running for cover, until the day she had no choice but to retreat to the deepest and darkest corner of your soul... where she still is today.

Now it's time to wake her up because you're going to need her strength and wisdom to pull yourself out of the hole you're currently in. You're drowning and she is waiting patiently on the shore with a life preserver, ready to throw it your way.

So, let's take those initial steps toward the truth, beginning with the reasons you chose this book and have read it thus far:

- You are in pain and you want to stop hurting
- You are ready to look at not only yourself but also those around you with complete honesty, specifically those you are loving or have loved and still feel emotionally connected to
- You are willing to accept that you are a beautiful and worthy being who makes this world better just by being in it
- You are willing to listen to the girl within who has a lot to say (after all, she's kept her mouth shut for a long time)
- And most important: You recognize that you are no longer alone

So take another deep breath, exhale, and even if your mouth won't participate, allow your soul for just this one moment to smile.

Because you're still that girl.

***

What's the greatest lesson a woman should learn? That since day one, she's already had everything she needs within herself, it's the world that convinced her she did not.
– Rupi Kaur

TRUTH BE TOLD

when we hide from the truth,
we hide from ourselves

"The truth does not change according to our
ability to stomach it emotionally."
– Flannery O'Connor

O oh, baby, this is a tender subject. But there's no getting around it. If you want to move forward and away from pain and suffering, you must travel through the truth to get there. Be prepared, however, because healing and recovering after heartbreak is in no way a linear process, especially when that heartbreak is driven by abuse. Think of it as a line from A to Z and you're going to jump in your car to get from one point to another. But when you sit in the driver's seat, you realize you have no key, and then your journey is over before it's even begun.

I hate it when that happens.

But wait! As you're feeling around in your pockets, looking through your purse or your entire house to no avail, that voice inside of you is reminding you where you left the key to your freedom – and it's with her, that girl, who by this point is tapping her foot with impatience while waiting for you to realize what you already know, which is that this truth is your key, and you're not going to get anywhere without it. There have been years where you thought you were going somewhere, but then just as many years when you found yourself in the same place again (the same kind of man, the same kind of friends) and unable to escape it no matter how much you try – the truth is stubborn like that and you can't drink it or eat it or smoke it or screw it away. That girl knows it, but she's kept quiet because she knew that this was a fork in the road you needed to find on your own.

Now that you're here, however, she's got your back for the way forward.

I wish I could tell you that there was a scenic route on this journey and that you could stop at the places that only felt and looked good, but the truth won't allow it because, frankly, it can get pretty ugly, like drop-down-on-your-knees-and-can't-get-up ugly. Like your-heart-is-going-to-implode ugly (especially when we deal with our illusions about the past). Because the truth, while being your key to freedom, won't hold back in its attempt to rip you wide open. It needs to do this so that you'll be left raw and exposed and vulnerable in a way you've never been before, knowing that this is the only place where the beauty of who you are and what you deserve will be found. As Rumi is famous for saying, "The wound is the place where the light enters you."

Like a birth, this process will test you, causing you to doubt if the pain will be worth it, but there is no other way for the light to get in and reach that girl inside of you who is begging for rescue. It's time. You've suffered long enough. You've given your power to people who never deserved it but who tricked and manipulated you into giving it to them. And now you sit alone and empty-handed, believing you're not worthy of anything better, believing others when they told you who you are.

As if they had a clue.

No one knows your brilliance, your wisdom, your courage, or your insight and instinct and intuition better than you, and the only reason you can't see this right now is because of the forgotten girl within. Here's what happened: You became a watered-down version of your true self. Faded. Colorless. Your life became a dimly lit room, with masks hanging all over it that you rotate depending on what your surroundings are demanding you to wear that day.

I hate that room. I lived in that room for a very long time. Some of the masks I wore included the nice girl, the obedient daughter, the submissive wife, the loyal friend, and of course – the one I hid behind the most – the silent bystander.

Since the truth was such a scary place to go, I spent decades avoiding it, which meant I spent a lot of time being silent. Whether it was with my emotionally abusive father, first husband, or second, I monitored everything that came out of my mouth to the point where not much ended up escaping because of the wrath I could possibly incur. Unbeknownst to me at the time, I had been training myself in the art of *speaking only when it's going to make the listener happy*. My father didn't like it when I expressed an opinion that he didn't agree with or when I in some way confronted him, and coincidentally neither did either of my husbands, who preferred it when I chose silence over challenging them in any way or bringing up issues they were averse to talking about. Thus, in my life over the course of three decades, the truth of my situation followed me around like a big white elephant that I pretended not to see as it filled up every room of my life and was the last thing I saw every night before I went to sleep when I whispered to the gentle giant, *Go away, you don't exist*. I purposefully avoided the truth, mainly because I didn't think I could handle it at the time. But that girl within me knew. In fact, she was often sitting atop that elephant, dozing off, like little girls do, when she grew bored waiting for me to come around.

She was always there, however, holding the truth in her hand like a precious stone. Call it instinct, intuition, a sixth sense – the semantics don't matter here. What matters is that we all have that voice of truth within us whether we choose to listen to it or not. That's why there are so many women who come to a point in their lives when they finally admit as they look on their past: *I knew it deep down. But I didn't want to know.*

I used to be that woman, but I got to a point where I didn't want to be her any longer because the pain was too awful to deal with over and over again. So at the age of forty-five, I made a conscious decision after escaping an abusive marriage to a diagnosed narcissist that I would rather feel the pain of the present than shove those feelings back down into the dark corner of my soul where the heartbreak wouldn't be able to breathe (like I did after my first marriage, which set me up for future failure). I knew that if I didn't feel it, *really feel it*, within every ounce of my being, then I'd only be intensifying the pain that would rear its ugly head at a later date. The way I felt when I initially left my marriage, or two months later or six months later, was not how I wanted to feel a year later or five years later. I didn't want to repeat whatever mistakes I had made that caused me to choke on my own shame, and I certainly didn't want to find myself in another similar relationship down the line. For example, back before I realized that girl was alive and well inside of me, I got away with throwing my hands in the air and giving up with the excuse, *I must be a magnet for horrible men*! Or worse, *I must deserve it*!

And let me tell you, nothing wakes up that elephant and the little girl sleeping on top of it like a trip into victimhood. That was the first time I remember hearing her voice. It was very faint, but still crystal clear: *Whoa. Now hold on there*, that girl warned. *Just who do you think you are?*

Was I really a magnet for the wrong kind of man? Did I actually believe that I did something bad in a previous life to have deserved the place I found myself in today? Or were these ideas just cop-outs that would conveniently release me from the responsibility of doing anything about it?

Ouch, that hurt. And that's exactly what I'm talking about when it comes to the truth – that moment when you realize you have more power than you think, when you can't run away from that girl within who continues to follow you everywhere (she was always particularly vocal with me at around two in the morning, though at the time I blamed my lack of sleep on my depleted adrenal glands). She's just not going to let you get away with your excuses anymore. She loves you that much.

In my own exploration of the truth after I escaped the darkness of my abusive marriage, here's what it looked like and what I needed to accept: I didn't have a target on my back, I didn't put out a want ad for an abuser to come into my life. I did, however, live and think in such a way that I opened the door for all kinds of abusers to walk in. This was part of the truth that both hurt like crazy but ended up setting me free so that I wouldn't repeat the same mistakes again. Because the fact is, we teach people how to treat us. That doesn't mean we deserve to be mistreated, though. So when we are, we need to pull ourselves out of the hole of blame and start looking at the facts, including how *the way we treat ourselves is in direct relation to how we are treated by others*.

I didn't deserve what happened to me, nor do any of us deserve to be mistreated or abused, but that's not the point if you want to move away from the pain and into the light of your new life, where love and hope and peace are waiting. The point is that there are facts and there are illusions about those facts. There are not two or three or four sides to your story; there is the truth. And in order to get to that truth, you must be open and willing to look at your own behaviors and thought patterns if you not only want to recover and heal but also want to avoid making the same mistakes in the future.

So what exactly is this truth I'm talking about? Is it about taking responsibility for your actions – or lack of – in the past? Yes. Is it about being responsible for the actions of others who hurt you? No. Is it about being honest with the choices you've made and why you made them? Absolutely. Is it about your faults that led someone you loved to treat you poorly? Not even a little bit.

The truth we're talking about is found in your treatment of the most important person in the world to you.

Now if you didn't immediately think of yourself as that person (and it's only natural that you might have thought of someone else, perhaps someone you love or your children – more on that later), then you've taken the first step in putting that key in the ignition and getting started on this journey of yours. So how about we get this honesty party started, shall we?

***

Women are especially hard on themselves, while excusing the men we love to the point it resembles a horror movie cliché when the audience is screaming at the girl, *Run!* while she continues to get that much closer to the ax-wielding psycho who is waiting for her around the next corner with full intent to do her harm. Meanwhile, the girl (who could easily have been me not long ago) is thinking, *Oh, he doesn't want to hurt me on purpose; he just had a bad childhood, or a bad day, or maybe his mother didn't love him, and if he does want to kill me, it's only because he loves me so much ...*

Admit it, it's tough to find any sympathy for her when she finally meets her ax.

Seriously, it's pathetic. And I used to be the queen of it, handing out Get Out of Jail Free cards to the people I loved – husband, father, friend – like nobody's business. In the meantime, I was a punishing overlord lacking any mercy when it came to myself. I took all the blame for my situation and stuffed it deep down inside where no one could see my utter humiliation at being a less-than-stellar human being. If the man I loved betrayed me, disrespected me, cheated on me, or in any way purposely broke my spirit in an effort to gain control, I immediately changed the direction of the pointed finger to the person whom I really believed was at fault: me.

My worthiness nonexistent, that girl within having been suffocated to a point where even had she shouted I wouldn't have heard her over the screams of my own condemnation, I became a stranger to myself. I believed what the man I loved told me: I was too emotional, too sensitive, too needy, too demanding, too this, and too that. Because of my sad state, no wonder he cheated on/lied/humiliated/ignored/insulted me. Somewhere in the darkest pit of my soul, I had begun to believe I deserved it, unaware that my beliefs about myself had been implanted by the very one I loved and trusted with my life.

To be clear, this self-loathing wasn't something I inherited. It wasn't in my DNA. I didn't go to school for it or buy it at the store. The reason I had no self-worth was a combination of two factors: I had someone whom I trusted condition me into thinking I was worthless so that I would continue to accept his abuse, and self-worth wasn't a concept I was familiar with. I had no clue about what it really was. I wasn't familiar with self-respect or boundaries or self-confidence because it wasn't something that I had any experience with growing up. Just like religion, money, or responsibility to our fellow man, in my house self-worth was never modeled, taught, or even talked about. As children, we lack the wisdom to inherently know that whatever takes place in our own home may or may not reflect the outside world. As children, we only know what we see and what we hear, and that information is usually offered in the form of a mom and/ or dad, maybe some older brothers or sisters, or an aunt or uncle who hangs around enough to be an influence.

I was the oldest child, sans any extended family, in a household where my father was demanding, bossy, easily angered, and sometimes mean and verbally abusive and who made decisions based solely on his own needs, which included everything from where we lived to what color to paint the living room wall to dictating our conversations at the dinner table each night. In contrast, my mother simply went along and made as little fuss as possible in order to avoid poking the bear (although bears were far less grumpy and my father far less dangerous). In addition, there was no affection in our home to offset the constant state of walking on egg-shells that my mother, my younger brother, and I were compelled to integrate into our daily lives. There was no "I love you" handed out, and the only hugs I remember receiving were on those rare occasions that demanded it such as at Christmas when a present was opened.

Now don't get me wrong. This isn't any sad Charles Dickens novel to describe my household growing up. I still enjoyed a great childhood. I have wonderful memories that sometimes include both my mother and father as I remember them in the good moments we shared as a family, such as on the rare occasion when we could get my dad to laugh or play with us. But these memories of mine are wonderful in spite of the lack of a healthy relationship between my parents. Unbeknownst to me at the time, I was forming my opinions about marriage, about how a husband treats his wife and how a wife responds, and about how men hold the power and women are lucky enough if they get a seat at the table.

Now if you were to ask my mom or dad about this, I'm fairly confident they'd deny any of this to be true since they have never enjoyed speaking about anything unpleasant if it pertains to them, and definitely not if they're challenged to take responsibility for it. At this point, I realize some may be uncomfortable with my opening up this closet of skeletons and bringing my parents into this. That's certainly not very nice of me (at least that's what my father would say).

I'm cool with that. Because here's the thing: We've been taught as women that naming and blaming is a game we ought to avoid playing. And wouldn't you know that's exactly how we get into trouble in our relationships. Suddenly we're changing the very core of ourselves to avoid being confronted about the way we truly feel inside, and we're made to feel bad about it when we express ourselves in a way that evokes rebuke from those who are listening. But this isn't about blame or shame. These are simple facts and have as much right to their telling as do the facts that are nonthreatening in nature – such as the fact that I went to Coconino High School or that my first car was an army green Dodge Demon or that I used to dunk my younger brother's toothbrush in the toilet when I was mad at him (I still to this day haven't told him, so *shhhh*).

This isn't my side of the story because this isn't a story. These aren't fairy tales I'm spinning; these are facts. So when I speak about this part of my life or any other part, I can reflect on it without bitterness, without anger, and without any emotional attachment whatsoever, which is crucial to our eventual healing and recovery after heartbreak. And that, my beautiful friends, is how the truth works its magic. No matter what happened to you in your past, the good and the bad have an equal right to exist since they both have shaped you into who you are today. Of course, I'm not talking about traveling to the past with the intent to literally change it (as my teenage son would say, *Yeah, duh!*) or with the intention of feeding any bitterness or regret. Instead, I'm talking about a more mathematical approach to viewing one's past: in the same manner in which we ask what two plus two is, we can ask ourselves such questions as "Why did I give him another chance to hurt me?" or "Why did I put up with it for so long?"

We need the answers to these questions or we are doomed to repeat our mistakes in the future. The past and the truth go hand in hand, and that girl within knows this all too well. She also knows that you're strong enough to handle it, even if you're not as confident yet in your own capabilities. But if you want to heal from heartbreak, if you want to recover from an abusive relationship, if you want to sever those emotional ties you have for someone who hurt you (and is still hurting you because of those ties), and if you want to move on from what is holding you hostage to what happened to you, then put that key to your freedom into the ignition, fire up the engine, and let's start our journey forward by going backward first.

Road trip.

BACK TO THE FUTURE
the past will help you heal the present

"Life can only be understood backward; but it must be lived forward."
– Søren Kierkegaard

There are endless amounts of clichés and sayings that make it sound like the past is a bad place and that the less time we spend there, the better. You've heard it a million times: The past is dead. Yesterday is history. Don't look back because you're not headed that way.

I'm calling that nonsense out (and so is that girl if you listen closely enough). I'm also calling out those who say such statements and exposing them as people who have something to hide, something to protect, or someone to control. One of the simpler reasons we know the past is very much alive is how it manifests physically for us: good memories trigger our endorphins, creating a sense of euphoria, while bad memories trigger stomachaches, cause our chest to tighten, or our sweat glands to open. And while we know the literal past cannot be changed, our feelings about it certainly can, which means we can change our body's physical reaction to our memories of it.

In American culture, we like to divvy up periods of time and pretend they stand on their own, disconnected from one another: the past, the present, and the future. That certainly does make it neat and tidy, as if life were a meal and the past is the appetizer, the present our main course, and the future our dessert (or stomachache, depending on how you spent your last supper). This would be a convenient way of looking at our past since we could pretend that once it's been chewed up, swallowed, and digested, it's left our body and will never return.

But our memories aren't food, they aren't a substance that is found outside of our body until we decide to bring them within. Our thoughts and feelings about the past are as much a part of our physical makeup as is the blood running through our veins. Though we were brought up on timelines (who *didn't* hate high school history class because of them?) and the idea that the road from birth to death is a straight shot, the passage of time is anything but a linear motion. Time itself is a continuum, without beginnings or endings, just like a circle. Even if someone dies, their time lives on in the memories of others – they don't just disappear for good as if they never existed. So, too, does the past continue because life isn't lived in a line. It's circular, a loop, a constant presence in our otherwise inconstant lives. As for the present moment, which will be different for you who are reading these words and me, who is writing them, it is true that the here and now is the only thing that exists, literally speaking. Yet, in the *now* in which we exist, when our hearts are beating and our cells are regenerating, so too our thoughts and emotions – based on past experiences – are playing an active role in the decisions and choices we make that will have a direct effect on our future.

This is why heartbreak caused by an abusive relationship is so difficult to recover from. All those memories we have are about events that happened in the past, but we feel them as though they are actually happening in the present. When I left my husband for the first time (like most victims, I did return to my abuser), I suffered deeply by reliving what had happened. I was unable to sever those emotional ties due to my attempt to sever the past from my present. My first mistake was trying to chop up time into those tidy little pieces I mentioned, believing that if I could leave my past behind and turn away from it as though it didn't exist, then I could move forward and away from the pain that threatened to destroy me. The problem with this scenario is that I was denying my soul the chance to reflect, to feel, and to grieve. I was denying that girl her right to breathe and have a say in what had happened. And this is where we get into trouble, that period after heartbreak and before recovery when we skip all the steps necessary to take care of ourselves and dive head first into the future without the safety net of emotional wisdom to save us. This place is trouble because we aren't making decisions from an authentic place of truth but instead from a place of pain that compels us to do anything possible to get rid of that pain. Some women jump right into another relationship, for example. Some return to the one who caused them to suffer in the first place (as I did). And some even drag their children along for the ride as they try unsuccessfully to make the pain disappear with behavior they later regret. All the while they are inflicting wounds on their children that are not so easily patched up.

This is what the process of recovering, healing, and moving on after heartbreak and abuse requires: looking honestly at how your past is affecting your present, which will in turn determine your future. This also requires a great deal of humility and sending your bruised ego into the corner for a time-out. I was dangerously close to losing myself in the deep pit of victimhood by focusing only on the thought of, *I didn't deserve this!* Especially right after I escaped my marriage the first time, when I spent hours collapsed on the floor and catching my tears in my open palms, heaving with sobs and feeling as though my heart would collapse from the pain – I couldn't move past this feeling of injustice that I had suffered. Of course, the tears and the time I spent on the floor unable to function were a necessary part of the grieving process that I needed to plow through, but spending that time thinking only of how I didn't deserve any of it was unproductive at best and dangerous at worst. The fact was that I *didn't* deserve what had happened to me, but this wasn't the point, and it was only when I could move away from that limiting belief to the wider space of understanding and truth that I was able to finally take those first baby steps on my journey to recovery.

If we spend all of our time focusing on our victimhood (*I didn't deserve this; I can't believe he did this to me; How could he!*), then we remain powerless to change our state of being. This is why the past, the truth, and that girl within can either serve as the greatest teachers we'll ever have or, if ignored, be our personal Bermuda Triangle where we'll be lost for good. Though it was one of the hardest things I've ever done in my life, accepting revelations about the true state of my marriage was what enabled me to later pick myself up off the floor, dust myself off, and get on with a life that had patiently been waiting for me. I had to come to terms with the fact that while my marriage looked solid and happy from a distance – and, boy howdy, did I spend a ton of my time convincing everyone else of this – up close it was a combination of codependency, willing blindness, manipulation, and abuse. Talk about a hard pill to swallow: it dawned on me one day that the past sixteen years of my life, spent with a man whom I had children with and had devoted my life to, were not as they appeared. That was the day the hole I had been digging for myself finally stopped growing and I threw the shovel away for good.

This journey of healing, however, was not one I could embark on alone. I needed the help and insight of the girl within who could remind me who I was, since I had lost myself somewhere along the way. Right before I left my husband for the second and final time, I was a shell of the woman I used to be. When I looked in the mirror, I didn't recognize who stared back at me. When I yelled at my kids, I didn't know whose temper that belonged to since my desire to be a good mother was the most important thing to me in the world. When I said nothing while the man I loved openly demeaned and disrespected me, I couldn't for the life of me figure out who this weak and pathetic woman was who put up with such a jerk. When I went out socially and stood next to my husband while he charmed and flirted his way through every vagina in a fifty-foot radius, I didn't know how my mouth was forcing a smile all on its own.

This is what the truth does to us if we deny its right to exist. Today I can see with crystal-clear precision the abusive relationship I was living – or I should say dying – within. Back then, because I had silenced that girl from my past who was definitely not OK with the pain I was feeling, I subconsciously put myself into an emotional coma so that any and all feeling – while I couldn't escape it entirely – would be at least dulled so I could get from sunup until sundown. This is how victims of all types of abuse, but specifically emotional abuse (and narcissistic abuse, more on that nightmare later), find themselves staying for years and years as they watch their former selves turn into someone they don't know. In addition, there is something that turns on a switch inside of us when we are not ready for the truth. We turn into our own expert defense lawyers overnight and work even harder to convince both others and ourselves that everything is peachy keen, like we're directing traffic around a fatal accident while assuring onlookers, "Nothing here to see, folks. Keep moving."

Here's where we locate that precious key we need to open the door necessary for us to move from here to there. And here's how that girl can help us find the courage to step through. The time is now to uncover the truth of how you ended up here, and do so without blame, without shame, just with some cold, hard facts about the past that until now you've been pretending don't exist (or maybe you've been trying to make them go away by self-medicating in some way, whether through alcohol or drugs or food).

I will promise you this: The truth will first kick you in the butt so hard you'll land flat on your back wondering what hit you. But then something glorious will happen. Instead of feeling like the one trapped in the cage with no way out, you will become a detached onlooker to your past. When I was living in the darkness, I felt as though I were looking at the world from the perspective of a trapped animal. Today, I feel like a scientist at the zoo, able to walk around and study all of the different animals of my past without any emotional attachment, knowing I'm safe because my past will never escape to hurt me again.

***

So now let's dig into one aspect of the truth that is necessary for our forward movement: the reality of how the one we loved treated us (or maybe is still treating us). I know, I know, he had his good days, right? So he lied again or cheated or hurt your feelings or disrespected you – what about all those other times when he was so loving and charming and wonderful, just like he used to be when you first met? That must prove something right there!

Now let's think back to feeling like that trapped animal who would be happy with the smallest of bread-crumbs tossed her way *because she's starving*. In this scenario, it's understandable that the person who tosses us those crumbs would appear to be our savior and the one who really cares about us. But in that moment, our thinking is muddled with desperation. In that moment, it is nearly impossible to see how we've been trained to lower our expectations to such a level that we are actually satisfied with crumbs, unaware that we deserve so much more. Narcissists in particular are masters at this tactic of "normalizing" a victim to the abuse. In essence, we are blinded by our own desperate need to get attention, love, and respect from the one we love to such a point that we can't see the truth right in front of us. We can't feel the chain around our neck as we're so focused on that meager offering of breadcrumbs that is designed to keep us in place, keep us under control, and keep us asking for more.

Here's how the past becomes a handy little tool when figuring out why we end up begging for crumbs from someone who had initially promised us a feast. The past will help us understand why we've confused love with abuse, and it will also help identify what real love is and what it actually looks like. What this process will do is help you take your love (or any remnants of love you still feel for the one who hurt you) out of the equation while you solve the bigger question of "How did I get here?" It's crucial to take your feelings and put them aside because you have work to do. Think of yourself as a detective who needs to uncover the clues needed to solve the mystery of where your self-worth disappeared to. This, in turn, will enable you to stop being a victim of abuse and start being a survivor of it.

It's time, Sherlock. Was it really love? Or was it abuse disguised as love? That girl within already knows, but she'll keep her mouth shut for now while you figure it out.

And she'll be right there with you, holding your hand along the way as you do.

WHAT'S LOVE GOT TO DO WITH IT?
why love and abuse cannot coexist

"Truth is like the sun. You can shut it out for a time, but it ain't going away."
— Elvis Presley

I spent sixteen years lavishing praise and admiration on my second husband. I was one of those annoying women who had only great things to say about the man I loved. To anyone who would listen, I told them what a great husband he was, what a fantastic father, a faithful and decent man who would never do anything to hurt me or our children. From the moment I met him, I was on his side. I believed everything he said. I was, quite literally, his biggest fan. So what if there were enough red flags in the early stages of our relationship to supply a Communist parade? I couldn't be bothered to listen to that nagging voice inside (*that girl* – who also wasn't fond of me calling her a nag) who was strongly advising me to run away and fast. What did she know anyway? Didn't I deserve a man who was so passionate and charming and who was obviously crazy about me? Besides, I hadn't listened to that girl for years at that point in my life, so I shut down all warning signals in my gut and listened only to my heart, which told me that I had finally found the man of my dreams. And there was no way I was going to let anything screw that up, especially logic, good sense, or something silly like the facts that framed the bigger picture of this relationship I was entering into. I couldn't risk losing the jackpot I felt I had won, so I muzzled that girl within and told her to go sit in the corner … where she stayed for the next decade while I kept pretending she didn't exist.

And that's where the real trouble began: that moment when I was so consumed with love that I could no longer see straight, my inner wisdom taking a sudden vacay. I looked the other way, I made excuses, I told myself that everything was just fine while avoiding facts, ignoring red flags, and continuing to trust that the one I loved was a good man whom I could rely on, despite all evidence to the contrary. The passing of time then numbed me to future red flags that popped up here, there, and everywhere. It's as if I had this beautiful green lawn in my front yard that I tended to and watered and cared for every single day, with my neighbors always commenting, *Wow your grass looks so great!* I was proud of my lawn. My happiness depended on it since I had an image to keep up, especially after working so hard to get it to that point and telling everyone how great it was all the time. When no one was looking, however, I started to notice these annoying dandelions (aka: the truth) popping up and then ended up spending the majority of my time pulling them out and discarding them before anyone noticed. It didn't take long before I was exhausted, unsure of how much longer I could keep up that emotionally draining charade. I was tired because weeding out the truth is backbreaking work, and before long it was all I was doing anymore: protecting my life and love as I knew it from imploding.

Why do so many of us do this for the ones we love? Especially when the signs are showing us along the way that something isn't right, that this marriage or relationship we've committed our soul to is not what it seems. This is the part of the truth that hurts the most when we start the process of healing. When I look back over the sixteen years I spent with the "man of my dreams," I can see clearly how I ignored a million and one signs, starting from the moment I met him (such as his cheating on a girlfriend with his good friend's wife, being fired from his managerial position for sexually harassing an employee, committing marriage fraud so he could stay in the country, and of course lying, lots and lots of lying). Remember when I said the truth would bring you to your knees? Well, once I admitted to myself how many warning signs I'd overlooked, I was broken to the point where I was so ashamed I had to avoid the mirrors in my home so I wouldn't have to look at my sorry self. This was a necessary butt-whooping, however, because then I could stand up, dust myself off, and look at the bigger picture of why I did this, which was crucial for my future since I never wanted to make that same mistake again. (Note: I am in no way saying that I deserved to be abused, only that there were lessons to be learned so that I wouldn't repeat the same mistakes in the future.)

Here's where my past – pre-husbands – helped me out. I realized that the fact *I had no boundaries established* regarding how others treated me put me into positions where I could be violated in all sorts of ways. Honestly, I didn't even know what a boundary was (except that it was an invisible line separating states) so how was I to enforce one? And why didn't I have boundaries established for my own personal safety? Well, as it turned out, I didn't think enough of myself to deserve any. Certainly no one ever told me I should have any. My father never once even hinted that I was someone who was worth something or had anything to offer, while my mother showed me by example that women simply had no right to defend or stand up for themselves. Because of this, by the time I met my first husband at the young age of twenty-two, I took all the love I had to offer and bequeathed it to him, saving not an ounce for myself (self-love is a prerequisite for setting boundaries). Then once I met my second husband – before even being divorced from my first – I simply transferred all that love I had to give onto him, like I was depositing all my money into his bank account while my own savings remained depleted. In other words, I made the men I married rich with my love while my own heart was flat broke.

Naturally, this opened the door for all sorts of trouble to come walking in.

Another mistake women often make when it comes to those we love is lowering our standards to such a level based solely on legality and the weight of a wedding certificate. I was guilty of this myself. I granted the one who held the title of "husband" a virtual free pass to get away with such behavior that I would never have tolerated from another human being. I made him my King while I filled my role as Queen of Excuses for the King: *He had a bad childhood. He's just misunderstood. He really doesn't mean to* [insert abuse here] *me. I just need* to [insert change to be made here] *and then he'll snap out of it.*

But they don't snap out of it. And there comes a point when we need to reevaluate what these labels such as "husband" and "wife" really mean and why we allow them to mean so much when our soul is suffering because of it. I was always concerned with being a good person and being nice, but what part of being good demands that we allow those who are not so good to hurt us? Because at that point of pain or suffering, everyone – spouse, family member, stranger on the street – needs to be on a level playing field. An abuser is an abuser, no matter if he put a ring on it.

***

This brings us to the point where a choice needs to be made on our part. Do we continue to shut up that girl within who is begging to be heard? Do we continue to yank those dandelions out of our perfect yard and hide them at all costs? Or do we fill up our depleted hearts with love for ourselves first so that we are prepared to open our eyes to the truth after having shut them for so long, after which we take the brave step of allowing that girl to come out of hiding and listen to what she has to say.

If you're sick and tired of avoiding the truth in your life, and you're ready to get back in touch with the one you can trust to help you see that truth so you can leave your pain behind you for good, then take a deep breath and get ready because that girl has some questions for you. And finally, after all you've endured, you're going to give her some answers.

She wants to know:

- Are you hurting because of someone you loved?
- Did the one you love hurt you without sufficient remorse? And do so repeatedly?
- Were you treated with respect and compassion at all times by the one you loved?
- When you expressed your pain, did the one you love listen? Care? Change?
- Did you feel completely safe with the one you loved?
- Were you certain that the one you loved would never hurt you on purpose?
- Do you love yourself enough to tell the truth about the one you loved?

These are the questions for which any answer requires the cold, hard truth. Whether you are still in some aspect of a relationship with the one you loved or not, these answers are crucial in your movement forward and away from your pain. If you can't be honest when you look back at your past, then your present and future will suffer because of it. Even if you've left the relationship far behind and vowed to never return, if there is any part of you still emotionally attached, then these questions will help clear up what it is about the relationship you made excuses for or had illusions about.

Sometimes the hardest part of healing and moving on is letting go of the dream. This is because while we're deep in any abusive relationship, we've trained our-selves to be less than truthful about our situation. Since I spent sixteen years weaving a fantastic tale of how great everything was in my marriage, ignoring the truth about a man who purposely inflicted pain in order to keep con-trol, it was imperative upon my escape to revisit all those memories and look at them honestly. This was definitely one of the hardest parts of my recovery, in that I had to admit there was a stark difference between what I wanted my marriage to be and look like, and what it actually was. In that first year after leaving, and then while going through the divorce process, I knew that if I tried to ignore the past and the state of my marriage, I would be doomed to repeat the same errors with another relation-ship in the future. And because of all the pain I had not only felt emotionally but physically as well (emotional abuse does a number on the physical body), I had come to a place where enough was enough. I was going to be honest about what *really* happened even if it killed me.

At this time, it needs pointing out that healing after an abusive relationship is a different animal altogether than healing after an otherwise healthy one. Not that there is any such thing as a "normal" divorce, but when two emotionally healthy people who have built a union on mutual respect decide to part ways, there is no need to pick apart their shared past because it's not affecting either of their futures. In otherwise healthy relationships, there are no rose-colored glasses to take off. In an abusive relationship, where a victim has been brainwashed into staying, for example, the past is a crucial piece of the puzzle in figuring out how to move forward. Victims of any kind of abuse (emotional, physical, financial, narcissistic) have often been conditioned, beaten down, manipulated, and deceived to the point where they don't recognize themselves in the mirror anymore. When I first left my marriage, I felt as though I'd escaped solitary confinement and was seeing the sun for the very first time. But here's the thing: It wasn't until I felt the sun on my face that I realized I had been living in the darkness. This is often the case with victims of abuse in that we don't realize we are victims until we've escaped and are looking at it in the rearview mirror.

And just like a prisoner being released after years of confinement, I had to relearn everything all over again. But first I had to examine my past so that I could then figure out the future. I needed the help of that girl because I didn't know who I was anymore. And if I couldn't recognize the woman in the mirror staring back at me, I knew she would. The tricky part of this period of time – after we've left but before we've purged those feelings toward the one we love – is figuring out how to examine the truth about our past and recognize the illusion for what it is, while at the same time feeling hurt and depressed because in many ways we're still in love to some extent. Of all the women I've spoken to and worked with over the years, this is the number-one mistake made when trying to recover from an abusive relationship: spending enormous amounts of our energy fighting this love we still feel for our ex.

That girls wants you to know: *This is why you cannot move on.*

The problem lies in the simple math of recovery. When we are badly hurt by someone we loved and devoted ourselves to (and may have had children with), there is only a finite amount of strength that we have available to pull from. Escaping an abusive relationship is already a hardship, one that mirrors the effect of having a hurricane rip through your home and leave you to pick up the pieces of a life you once lived but is now decimated. Afterward, there is only so much time in the day to clean up, assess, and figure out what the next step will be.

Trying to recover and heal from an abusive relationship requires no less of your time and energy. If you spend those moments, however, trying to fight your feelings for your ex (especially if you've only recently left or been left), then you are taking precious time away from yourself and redirecting it to the one who hurt you in the first place. It's the same story I hear over and over again: *I don't know what to do because I still love him!* This single statement explains why a woman returns to her abuser an average of seven times. The problem is found in whatever feelings we still have for the one who hurt us. If there's still love there, we think it's a sign that either we're meant to go back or that we made a mistake. On top of that, we pile the guilt on ourselves because we still love the person who we know full well has hurt us intentionally, and we're riddled with shame because what does that say about us if we still have feelings for our own abuser?

It comes down to a matter of energy. If you want to heal and move forward and away from a life of pain and suffering, you must fully commit to your own well-being and stop extending your energy in any other direction than to yourself. This means to drop the guilt of still being in love with the one who hurt you and instead focus on the reality of the future, which promises that time will take care of that love you feel and it will dissipate eventually on its own. Like a plant that's not watered, any love will lose its breath and wilt underneath the light of your new life until it disappears altogether. I promise, any love you carry will not last. And once that love has left your system and you're ready, then and only then will your heart be wide open for real love to come into your life.

So go ahead and feel that love for your ex. Let that love just sit there and be inside of you while you keep yourself occupied with putting one foot in front of the other and continuing to move forward and into a life that you always dreamed of and that you deserve. Don't fight what you feel because fighting saps your strength, and when we are recovering from such pain, we need all the strength we can get. It's also crucial to remind yourself every time you start feeling a pull of love that tempts you to move backward in any way at all, that this love you feel is the same you felt while you were in the relationship and *it didn't cause you any less pain*. In fact, it probably caused you to suffer even more because your love was not returned as it should be. The truth is that love doesn't hide itself within abuse, so any love you're feeling post-escape is only a reflection of the desperate attempt to keep the illusion of the relationship alive.

Bottom line, accept your feelings for your ex, know that they won't last forever, and turn your attention toward the one who really needs all the love you can give at this point: Yourself.

UNDERSTANDING THE LANGUAGE OF NARCISSISTIC ABUSE
yes, narcissists do it on purpose

> *"The narcissist devours people, consumes their output, and casts the empty, writhing shells aside."*
> – Sam Vaknin

A t this point, you might still be skeptical as to whether or not you've been (or are) a victim of abuse. This is a natural reaction considering our society has convinced us to believe that (a) abuse consists only of bruises and broken bones, (b) marriage is hard work so if you're unhappy it's your own fault and no the grass isn't greener on the other side, and (c) women aren't worthy enough to expect to be treated with respect and dignity at all times. Combine this with the fact that many of us grew up with parents who were to some degree enforcing this thought pattern that men are inherently worthier than women, then it's pretty easy to see why so many victims of abuse don't even realize they are victims.

Narcissistic abusers in particular are masters at their game, and in many respects it is easy for them to find their prey considering that so many of us women are unwittingly lured into their traps because of our empathetic and forgiving nature. This is in addition to the fact that so many victims of abuse come from backgrounds that have enforced their unworthiness, and an abuser simply takes advantage of those foundations and uses them to gain the upper hand. It's important to point out that abuse does not abide by any gender or race or class. There are female abusers just as there are male victims. However, since the majority of abuse victims are female and the majority of abusers are male, I will focus on that relationship since how we view men and women in society has everything to do with why these statistics are as they are.

Here's where that truth pops up again and where that girl can help you out, since no one but her has the inside scoop on what you experienced growing up, which will help explain how you ended up where you are today. Once I followed the breadcrumbs back to the very beginning – literally to when my memory started – the men

I chose later on made all the sense in the world. I grew up with a father whose needs were constantly required to be met by my mother. Her needs were inconsequential. Her dreams, her desires, even her basic necessity for love and compassion that all humans share was delegated to the lowest rung on our family's ladder. As the only daughter in our family of four, I subconsciously absorbed these behaviors playing out in front of me to the point where they became part of the narrative I told myself when I was older. In addition, my father never in any way reacted toward me as though I were something special to him. At no time during my childhood or fragile teenage years did I feel that I was of any worth to him, and his attention was impossible to get unless I got into trouble. Therefore, I got into a lot of trouble since any attention was better than none. The problem with this scenario, however, was that this became our only way of interacting – I got into trouble and then he told me what a troublemaker I was and that I should be embarrassed and ashamed and how could I do that *blah blah blah*. And yet, there was still some part of me that was satisfied because I had, ultimately, gotten his attention.

My lack of self-worth was also reinforced by having a mother who avoided confrontation at all costs, and who was unable to not only stand up for herself but also for her children. When I think back to the role my mother played in my youth (she was a very loving mother, she just struggled with her own issues that got in the way of her helping her children with theirs) I always envision her as a lamp without a bulb, unable to shed any light and trying to take up as little space as possible. No matter what was said – or shouted – between my father and me, she had nothing to say about it. She also wasn't one to come behind the scenes to comfort or console me. She didn't offer any uplifting words or advice that might make me realize I was worthy or special, despite what my father said. This Bermuda Triangle of family dynamics then followed me once I turned eighteen and left home. And it is exactly what led me to dive head first into two abusive marriages that would last decades.

Here is where that girl helped me out after I left my second husband and began the long road of recovery: She is the one who showed me the pattern of emotional abuse in my family, because I would never have seen it for myself. As far as I was concerned, my dad wasn't abusive because he didn't hit any of us. I had been indoctrinated to accepting his emotional, financial, and narcissistic abuse as normal as though all families were like this. And society backed me up by constantly telling me that women weren't worthy of anything better. Marriage was a commitment that you needed to keep at all costs, and if it wasn't working, then you needed to toughen the heck up and maybe keep your mouth shut while you're at it. In and around this idea, there is a list of expectations women must contend with, such as the notion that women need to "take one for the team," meaning there exists an unspoken reality that within a heterosexual couple there should be only one speaker, which ultimately must be the man since a woman isn't as reliable and could potentially go off the rails with her tendency to be too emotional. And nobody wants that. This imbalance of expectations between husbands and wives, fathers and mothers, boyfriends and girlfriends is the underlying cause of our acceptance of abuse as a whole. The list of expectations for women – specifically wives and mothers – is so long it makes the Bible seem like a quick read, while conditions put forth for a man could be summed up on a sticky note. I'm guilty of following this rulebook myself while letting the men in my life off the hook. While women in general are expected to check all the boxes and balance balls on their nose in the futile attempt to be a good wife and/or mother, men are applauded if they just show up somewhere unexpected, like at a park to play with their kids (you know we've all seen that guy and said, *Oh, what a great dad!* while the other twenty moms in the same park remain unnoticed).

Now I'm not bashing the dads of the world who really are great (and there are far more great ones than not), but it's necessary to point out our collective opinion and judgment about men and women, along with the differences, so that we can get a clearer picture of why in our own lives this may be playing out in the form of abuse. These hypocrisies are exactly what lead us into relationships where we are getting the short end of the stick, where we are not having even our most basic human needs met, and the one we love is able to carry out his abuse while we silently endure it. To add insult to injury, we end up normalizing abuse when it doesn't come with physical violence attached. So maybe we'd leave if the one we love actually hit us (the key word being "maybe"), but it's OK to demean, disrespect, lie to, cheat on, and manipulate us?

Even if you're not experiencing the abuse firsthand anymore, even if it's now in your past whether that be a month or a year or several years, the key to your recovery is in understanding how the process of abuse happened so that you can avoid similar relationships in the future and also finally let go of that blame and shame that you're currently holding on to and which is killing you slowly. The fact is, *love does not hide itself within abuse*. The problem is, in the beginning of any abusive relationship (but especially with a narcissist), it appears to be just the opposite. When I used to look back on the first few years with my second husband, I glowed with memories of his adoring love and passion that he showed me. So much so that when the abuse became more regular, I had already conditioned myself to believing he was my Prince Charming and could do no wrong and that he loved me. Think of a frog in a pot of cool water (it's a much-used analogy, but a good one). The frog is just hanging out, doing what frogs do, totally oblivious to the fact that someone has turned the stove on to boil. Thus, by the time the water has actually begun to heat up and then bubble, it's too late for the frog to escape; it has already been cooked enough to render it helpless. This is the normalization of abuse, and narcissists are masters at it.

***

What Does Narcissistic Abuse Look Like?

The term *narcissist* is all the rage lately and it seems like everyone can be called one at this point. But don't get caught up in the myths and hype surrounding this term or believe that it's a simple case of staring at yourself lovingly in the mirror or taking too many selfies. Narcissistic abuse, while not physically visible, is capable of causing intense damage and trauma while leaving what can be lifelong scars on the hearts and souls of its victims. For example, a narcissist will drain you, emotionally, financially, or both. One moment you'll be swinging from the heavens from his adoration and love, and the next you'll be looking up from the fiery depths of purgatory wondering what happened. You'll be showered in love and affection until you're smothered by cruelty that will ask you to give him everything while demanding that you expect nothing in return. Narcissistic abuse is a dark and confusing tunnel where victims might spend years not realizing what is happening, unaware that their abuser has purposely created a world to isolate, demoralize, and dehumanize their victims to better feed and supply their disorder. Because of this, escaping a narcissist and recovering after such abuse is equally harrowing in that a reflection on the past – no matter how much it hurts – is necessary to move forward. Healing after narcissistic abuse is no small task and must be looked at like a puzzle. You cannot free yourself from the pain and emotionally detach until each piece is put back into place so that you can see the full picture of what happened to you.

Some of the emotions a victim of narcissistic abuse may feel after leaving the relationship include guilt, self-blame, confusion (living in a fog), and rage. This makes sense considering that a victim has in essence been brainwashed to such an extent that she no longer knows what's up or down anymore. In the last few years of my marriage, I remember feeling crazy and that everything was all my fault. I drowned in shame and often stared for extended lengths of time into the mirror at the dark circles under my eyes and the loss of light within them. I didn't know who I was anymore and didn't realize that the one person I loved more than anything in the world had systematically and purposefully trained me into believing these things about myself. Recovering afterward, therefore, required a purposeful retraining of my thought processes, but only after admitting that I was a victim of abuse so that I could move forward into becoming a survivor.

The truth is that love does not live in this darkness. Your love for your abuser may have felt very real, but that love was based on an illusion. Likewise, your abuser did not feel love because love is not a tool used to hurt or control another human being. I know that in the beginning it seemed everything was so perfect and beautiful, but the truth (and that girl within) knew it was an illusion all along. But that's the talent of a narcissist – they know what they're doing and how to get you hooked. It doesn't matter how strong or smart you are, only that you're an empathetic and loving soul who trusts in the good in people and believes in love. A narcissist's seduction is that he knows this about you, and he knows how smart and strong and passionate and beautiful you are, which is why he picked you in the first place. Of course, they're not going to *show* you who they really are in the beginning of the relationship or you wouldn't have given them a second date. Narcissists are master manipulators and will win you over in the beginning by love-bombing the heck out of you, grooming you, normalizing their behavior and gaslighting you so that you will allow their abuse to continue.

At this point, that girl you used to be is holding your hand right now as you dive into the realization that you may very well have been a victim of narcissistic abuse. But there's no other way than *through*, so let's take a deeper look into your past and see if we can't clear some stuff up so you can put a few more pieces of that healing puzzle into place.

How to Identify a Narcissist in Your Life

Let's start with the basics, specifically with the definition of narcissistic personality disorder. Let me clarify that whether the one who broke your heart is ever professionally diagnosed as a narcissist (as my ex was) is irrelevant in that your healing is not dependent on their diagnosis. You know your experience better than anyone else. You have what I call "street cred" – meaning that you don't need a master's degree to know what you've been through. Anyway, there are plenty of therapists who have their degrees and are still clueless about narcissists and the damage they do to their victims. You know who does have all the answers for you? That girl. So listen to her as you read through the next few pages.

An individual with narcissistic personality disorder has a distorted self-image, unstable and intense emotions, is overly preoccupied with vanity, prestige, and power, lacks empathy, and has an exaggerated sense of superiority.

There is a language surrounding narcissistic abuse that will help empower you to recognize it, understand it, and therefore use it as a tool to help you recover and heal from it. Also, as in my own experience, it will arm you with the knowledge needed so that in the future you will be able to spot a narcissist coming from a mile away. Because life's too short to spend even one more minute in the presence of one.

Love-Bombing

Remember that frog in boiling water I told you about? Well, the way it got in the pot in the first place is because it was love-bombed, which can be defined as *a manipulation tactic involving lavish demonstrations and constant bombardments of attention and affection in an attempt to gain control by moving the relationship forward quickly.*

I was that frog. I fell hard and I fell fast, jumping in headfirst without blinking, believing him after only months of dating when he declared his never-ending love and that I was his soul mate, that I had brought meaning into his meaningless existence. He drowned me in passion. He couldn't keep his hands off me. We made love often, sometimes up to five or six times a day. He wrote me notes, poetry, recited poems in public, told everyone that I would be his wife and that I was the mother of his unborn children. I didn't have time to think, to reflect, to question. There was nothing I could do but free fall into his love and ride it like a roller coaster with my eyes squeezed shut – I was scared to death but I still didn't want to get off. Looking back, I can see now how that girl was watching me all along while screaming *What do you think you're doing?* But I ignored her. She was simply no match for my amazing new man.

Here's where the truth of my past came back to bite me in the butt. The reason I fell so hard and so fast was because I didn't have the necessary self-worth and boundaries to warn me that any relationship that starts so quickly is one bound to fail. Love doesn't work like that. Love takes its time to grow. Love doesn't have a motive. There is no need for love to "trap" you and make sure you don't get away. Narcissists, however, have all the motive in the world to set you up for a future of accepting abuse. That's why they move so fast in the beginning. They know their mask is going to eventually fall off, so why not brainwash you into believing they're wonderful by the time that it does?

Grooming

Grooming is a calculated tactic by a narcissist of maneuvering a person into a more dependent and isolated position by claiming a "special connection" where a victim is more vulnerable to accepting future abusive behavior. Like a predator on the hunt, a narcissist will train you to be his, to fall for him, to love him, to accept him, to the point where you love him more than you love yourself. Why is this important to recognize? Because your full healing will require the understanding that you were his prey and therefore innocent of what he had in store for you and what came next.

Speaking of prey, narcissists hunt for empaths: *highly sensitive people who often take on the emotions of others at the expense of their own well-being.* I was a prime target for my ex because I was full of forgiveness and understanding, having grown up with the belief that all people were essentially good. Because of this belief, I traded listening to my gut instinct (that girl) and trusted the man I loved instead. This way I could make excuses for his bad behavior and accept all of his apologies when he did something that hurt me. The problem was that he kept repeating behaviors that hurt me and kept repeating his apologies. This is easy to do for a narcissist because they are inherently pathological liars.

This is another piece of the puzzle we can plop in that starts to fill in the bigger picture of the illusion any victim of narcissistic abuse lives within.

The Difference Between a Mistake and Narcissistic Abuse

If an emotionally healthy person you love ends up hurting you in some way, he will make immediate amends to correct his mistake to ensure it won't happen again because he loves you and cares about you and would never intentionally hurt you. With a narcissist, however, he may apologize or not (many never apologize for anything and make you feel at fault for their mistakes), but it doesn't change his behavior. He just needs you to shut up about it so that he can continue with his abuse. The phrase "actions speak louder than words" is a mantra to adhere to when dealing with narcissists. Don't listen to what they say because they are incredibly crafty with words and you don't stand a chance. Watch what they do, and then do again, and then again and again. When I look back on the sixteen years I spent with my second husband, I can see clearly the pattern that was established from the very beginning of him erring in some way that brought me pain to some degree and the repetition of that behavior as the years went by. He had no remorse and, in fact, only got better over the years of convincing me that I was the one with the problem ("You need to stop living in the past" was his favorite expression to guilt-trip me with). Therefore, once I escaped and began my journey of recovery, I felt backlogged with all those years of his misdeeds that I had never been validated for.

That girl let me know: I needed to let that all go because I was never going to get closure from a narcissist. It's just not going to happen. This is where we can slip into victimhood a bit easily, that point where we really want to be vindicated for what happened to us.

But here's the thing: to move from victim to survivor you need to vindicate yourself because no one else is going to do it for you. Yes you were wronged, yes you were harmed, yes they did it on purpose, and no they'll never admit it. But here's the good news: *You're not the narcissist!* You are a loving and compassionate and beautiful human being who will one day again reap all the rewards that love and life have to offer. A narcissist will never have that (and don't even believe for a second that they're happy without you and succeeding in their new life – it's all a charade and they desperately need you to buy it) because narcissists are filled with shame and are inherently cowards, which is what drives them to abuse so freely. So, congratulations on being a good person!

Gaslighting

Another sign that you were a victim of narcissistic abuse: Do you doubt your own memory of what occurred? Still can't recognize the woman in the mirror? That, my friends, is a product of gaslighting, a narcissist's favorite tool to make you feel like the crazy one while they stand back with a smirk on their face and watch their handiwork unfold in the form of your undoing. *Gaslighting is a form of mental abuse that includes brainwashing or convincing a mentally healthy individual that their understanding of reality is false, and makes victims doubt their own memory, perception, and sanity;*

the term is from the 1944 movie Gaslight *in which the villain uses this technique.*

This is part of the reason that you feel like you're taking ten steps back for every step forward in your attempt at recovery and healing after an abusive relationship. You're still convinced at some level that you're not all there. Again, the good news is that once you know how you've been manipulated, deceived, and brainwashed, you can begin the process of retraining yourself to tap into the strengths of that girl so she can remind you of who you used to be. Despite what you've been told or accused of, you're not crazy, you're not too emotional, you're not too sensitive, you're not dumb or weak or unstable in any way whatsoever. You are simply a person who has experienced incredible trauma at the hands of someone you loved, and no one can fault you for that.

The way that you're going to thrive after suffering at the hands of a narcissist is through your own empowerment, education, and enlightenment. It's time for you to recognize the exquisite being you are, to tend to your open wounds, to take a deep breath and hug yourself through the exhale, to let the tears fall and catch them with your open palms, and to finally, after all this time spent in pain and suffering, forgive yourself for actions inflicted on you that were never your fault in the first place.

It's time to remind yourself of how much love you have, what that looks like, and how no one in the world is more deserving of that love than yourself.

REAL LOVE DOES NOT ABUSE
*how he treats you is
how he feels about you*

*"Love is patient, love is kind. It does not envy,
it does not boast, it is not proud. It does not
dishonor others, it is not self-seeking, it is not
easily angered, it keeps no record of wrongs."*
– 1 Corinthians 13:4–5

I read once that we should replace the word "love"
in the above passage with the name of who it is we
love and see if the words still ring true. I can tell you
that I put in the names of my first and second husband,
as well as my father, and *surprise surprise* I couldn't
even get through the first sentence with any of them.
Of course, I never could do anything about my father
and how he treated me, but it was a necessary wake-up

call when I realized that the men whom I had loved and devoted myself to, and even had children with, would never reciprocate that love in return since the fact is that *true love does not abuse.*

This is such a turning point when we're recognizing the illusion of our past relationship because how else are we to move forward if not to do so honestly and authentically? The other illusion that is necessary to accept is that of our perception of whom we loved (or still love in some way). Abusers, and narcissists in particular, do not present themselves as they are. Their lives are a charade, a circus, and they are the ringmaster. Any victim is in the front row of their one-man show. Therefore, one of the truths we must admit to ourselves is that we bought a ticket to that show for a long, long time (some of us longer than others). Here is another opportunity to face the truth head on even when it hurts. I remember feeling like I had been punched in the stomach whenever I realized another truth about myself and the man I loved for so long. Why does it hurt so much? Because we feel like suckers, we feel like fools, we feel stupid and weak and pathetic for having fallen for such an act. Coupled with any love we still feel that we're somehow unable to stop feeling, and the shame can be overwhelming, which is why so many women decide to avoid the hard part of healing and jump straight into another relationship or self-medicate so they no longer feel the pain. I know this may not sound like good news, but any pain and suffering we experience while we're traveling *through* the healing process (opposed to avoiding it altogether) is designed to shape us into stronger and more resilient beings afterward who can fully embrace our place in the light and the life we always deserved to live.

First things first: Think about the one who broke your heart. Do you still love him? Do you still think about going back? Do you still wish it was like it used to be when you thought you were happy? It's important that you recognize who you're really still loving and/or missing. Is it really him or are you missing the man he pretended to be? Or the man you wanted him to be. Was he really loving you or *was he killing you*? When you think back on your relationship or marriage in its entirety (not just the good times), do you remember how he treated you in each of those moments? What exactly are you missing anyway?

Remember (and this is good to know for any relationship with anyone moving forward): *How he treats you is how he feels about you.* So, if he is kind and wonderful and loving 50 percent of the time, what does that say about how he really feels about you when the other 50 percent comes attached with your pain and suffering? The reason it's necessary to be clear on this image you have of your ex is because illusion will be the emotional death of you. Your illusions of others are the reason you found yourself in an abusive situation in the first place (as I did, but I've already had my come-to-Jesus moment with the truth so I can speak freely about this now). This does not mean, however, that you must attempt to cease all feelings for your ex immediately. That too will have disastrous consequences, as I explained before using the hurricane analogy when you have only so much energy to pick up the pieces and move forward into your new normal.

This is a good point to remind you of what exactly a healthy relationship – and healthy person – looks like so that you'll have something to compare to when looking back. A person who is emotionally healthy and not abusive will not play mental games at your expense. He won't leave you walking on eggshells wondering what mood he's going to be in, nor will he possess a Jekyll/Hyde personality that leaves you guessing who will walk in the door every day. Sure, he'll make mistakes, but he won't intentionally cause you harm, and if he does hurt you he'll do everything in his power to remedy it and make sure to not make the same mistake again. *A healthy person who loves you does so with integrity and will not leave you questioning that love on a regular basis.* He will honor you as you are, not who he thinks you should be. And above all, he will be your partner in life – not your father, not your psychiatrist, not your boss, and certainly not your enemy.

This is the type of relationship you've always deserved. Now that you're starting to realize it, it's time to face all those feelings you have for the one who never deserved you in the first place.

***

If what you're feeling is not love but anger, even rage, it's important to still let that girl scream her head off if need be. Trauma has a way of permanently changing us to the point where we're forced to create a new normal. This is a tough truth to accept but accept it we must. And part of that new normal is allowing for full expression of our feelings of the past. When I was fresh out of my marriage and going through the divorce process, I would cry so hard that I couldn't pick myself up off the floor; then I would feel so much rage at what had happened that, let me just say, it was a good thing my ex was nowhere in the near vicinity because who knows what would have happened. My emotions seesawed between hopelessness, sadness, anger, and rage to the point where I could feel all of those things within a few moments time. I moved back and forth between being a helpless heap on the floor to feeling empowered in my new life to hating myself for getting into this mess in the first place to hating him for all the ways he had hurt me. Though the journey was the hardest

I'd ever experienced in my life thus far (I would have rather given birth ten times over than go through that sort of pain) it was this exact process of purging and feeling all of my emotions that led me to eventually crawl out of the hole I was in and not only see the light again, but feel it hold me in a warm embrace knowing that my life would forever be changed for the better because of it.

So whatever stage you're at in your healing process, remember that the girl within is also hurting. She needs to grieve, so allow her the room to feel the pain and push through it. Allow the tears to fall until you're soaked from them, but don't let them fall in vain. That girl doesn't want you to drown. Think of the grieving process as modern poet Rune Lazuli explains: "Each tear is a poet, a healer, a teacher."

Now it's time to get crystal clear on the difference between love and abuse disguised as love. This is tough because it requires our utmost honesty in looking back and coming to terms with the fact that our abuser did not love us, and – this is a tough one to swallow – *we also didn't love them*. We loved the illusion of them and who we thought they were (which was not our fault; we were duped).

I'm going to spell this out and make it really easy to understand. There is no wiggle room here, no room for excuses or talking ourselves out of it. Because love does not abuse. Full stop.

What Does Real Love Do?:

- It opens its arms and embraces you without conditions
- Real love is the water and you are the flower; you will never die of thirst
- It keeps its promises, is humble and forgiving, and expands with your happiness
- It is a campfire that never goes out and will always keep you warm
- It lights up when you walk in the room and misses you when you're gone
- It makes mistakes but doesn't repeat those mistakes, especially if they hurt you
- It expands with your growth; it wants to see you succeed
- It enables you to sleep well at night knowing that you are safe in its arms

What Real Love Doesn't Do:

- It does not ask you to make yourself smaller so it can take up more space
- It is not threatened by your brilliance or your ability to change and adapt
- It does not ask you to stop shining your light or force you into the darkness
- It does not ask you to shrink so that it may stay comfortable

- It does not demand your silence
- It is not insecure, needy, or devious; it doesn't scheme, bully, or deceive
- It won't kick you when you're down; it won't blindside you
- It doesn't talk behind your back; it doesn't lie about you to others
- It won't take up all the air in the room while you suffocate in the corner

And finally, real love won't mask itself in an illusion that is of our own creation. No matter how long we make excuses for someone who is purposely inflicting pain, no matter how many apologies we accept, no matter how many mistakes we overlook or how many crimes we forgive, our desperate search to find real love within an abusive relationship is a dead end. Because real love does not exist within the darkness of abuse, it simply cannot exist in the same realm as power and control of another human being. The love we feel for the one who is hurting us may be real, but it is not being returned and therefore cannot wholly exist in the presence of another's debasement.

Real love soars and is the wind beneath our wings, while abuse disguised as love sinks and brings us to our knees. Real love is full of integrity, character, and serves our best interests, while abuse disguised as love will lie, cheat, and steal until we are reduced to nothing and can't pick ourselves up off the floor.

But you don't need me to tell you any of this.

You don't need a list or to check off what applies one by one. You already know because that girl knows. So if you've been fighting the truth of your situation or of your past then it's only because you didn't yet want to know. The facts are laid out clearly for you to see. Now is the time of accepting them and getting ready to leave this pain far behind you and find your way to the light – where real love is waiting for you.

CLEANING HOUSE
kick everyone out
of your headspace

"The two most powerful warriors are patience and time."
– Leo Tolstoy

"Why can't you just move on?"
"Why did you stay with him?"
"Why didn't you leave sooner?"

Nothing is more damaging to a victim of abuse than being asked one of these shame-filled questions. In addition, you have those who might not mean to hurt you but are doing so anyway when they say things like "You need to let the past go" or "You need to forgive. You know … so you can *move on*."

Honestly, I'm not sure what drives certain people to get into other people's business and tell them how to live their life, especially when a non-victim of abuse tries to counsel an actual victim. Whatever the case, I'm here to tell you right here and right now that you will hear, if you haven't already, such victim-shaming on a regular basis during your healing journey. So let's just agree that they don't deserve one ounce of your time or headspace so that you can get back to the business of recovery, OK?

In addition to these loud voices that come straight out of the mouths of people you may come across, there are also those voices that live in your head that will cause you constant grief if you don't recognize them right away (such as the voice that whispers: *Maybe he was right and you ARE pathetic* or *You'll never find anyone better*). These voices from your past are not yours by a long shot, but after what you've been through you've probably convinced yourself that they are. For purposes of healing, it's important for you to both figure out whose voice belongs to whom and also make the voice of that girl a priority and listen to her and only her in times of doubt, reflection, and circumspection. The reason is because everyone else, including the voices from your past that live in your head, do not have your best interests in mind. Hence when those voices are coupled with the voices of your friends, family, or even strangers, it makes it all but impossible for you to move forward. Why? Because people who have not experienced abuse, especially narcissistic abuse, have no clue what you've been through and therefore have no clue about how you should recover. There are those who may have good intentions when they tell you to just "move on," or who simply can't comprehend why you won't let the past go and stop all feelings about it immediately, but the reality is that anyone who is unfamiliar with abuse and narcissists and who tries to "help" you is no different from a person who doesn't know Spanish trying to teach you how to speak it.

The voices in your head are the ones that do far more damage, mainly because you've been listening to them for so long that you think they're yours. In fact, the only voice that is yours is that girl, and you stopped listening to her a long time ago. Or maybe you listen but then allow another voice to speak over her. Trust me, I've ridden in this rodeo so I know the feeling. The key to your complete healing, however, is dependent on recognizing who lives in your head and whose advice you're taking. Since I'm a child of the 1970s and '80s, I always think of the voices in my head as cassette tapes that self-rewind and then hit playback. Once I recognized this, though, it was easy to see how so many voices from my past had been influencing my decisions of my present simply by playing themselves over and over again. For example, everything that my first and second husbands told me about myself (they had a lot in common in that respect) – *You're too emotional, too needy, too sensitive, too high maintenance* – was on replay to the point where I began believing these things about myself and therefore impeded my own healing after ending each marriage because I was stuck in my presumed weaknesses. In any abusive relationship, an abuser uses words as a weapon in order to keep a victim quiet, subdued, and under control. Whenever I voiced an opinion or stood up for myself with either of my ex-husbands, they used words to put me back in my place so they could maintain their position of power. And nothing shuts a woman up like telling her she's too emotional or too sensitive since that's such an awful thing to be (or so we've been trained to believe).

The other problem with listening to the voices in our head when we're trying to heal is that the main voice is typically from our abuser, who has to some degree or another conditioned us over time to accept his abuse. This tactic of making a victim feel terrible about herself, combined with the method of gaslighting, inevitably convinces her of her unworthiness, which continues long after the relationship is over. So the first thing you must do, no matter where you're at on your road to recovery, is to recognize those voices in your head. I wish I could tell you that they'll just go away once you do, but since it took a long time for them to be implanted it takes a long time for them to go away. The key is to recognize the voice, greet it (I say something like, "Oh, hello, Dad" or "Hello, X" or if I'm in a really snarly mood, "Back again, Scumbag?"), and then let it firmly know that it has no business in your head, it's wrong about you, and frankly it can go *insert favorite expletive here* itself. After all, the one who broke your heart has full knowledge of your brilliance and also knows that you're going to not only be fine without him but better off, which is why those words he used to put you down and shut you up still have such power.

Never underestimate the power of words. That old saying "sticks and stones may break my bones but words will never hurt me" is a boatload of bull manure. For years in my second marriage I used to wish that he would hit me instead because the brutal pain of his words was too much to bear and then at least I'd have something to show for my suffering. The pain of his words was so intense at times that it had a far worse impact on my physical body than an actual punch in the stomach ever would. Imagine how much pain someone must be in to wish for a bruise or black eye – or maybe you don't have to imagine it because you've felt that way yourself? Of course, I'm in no way insinuating that physical abuse is any better, but instead pointing out that emotional abuse is just as painful if not more so mentally speaking.

These voices from your past (and that girl knows who said what and when so it's a good idea to listen to her since she's been keeping notes) also transform into labels that you end up wearing for your entire life if you never recognize them. Think of them like sticky notes. For example, when I was young, I believed I could do anything. I wasn't yet held back by the fact that I was a girl. My dreams were gargantuan. My courage unrelenting. My spirit soared and I truly believed I could fly or walk into wardrobes in search of Narnia if I wanted to (I actually tried both more than a few times). Then there came that point when people started putting labels on me. By the time I was an adult I had taken these words, these accusations, these descriptions that claimed ownership and branded me, and believed them to be my own. I believed them to be true. I believed in their internal existence, when in actuality their power was only in my own submission to their external adherence to my being.

Whether it was my father, a husband, a friend, a stranger, or society – I had collected these sticky notes over the years to the point where I could barely breathe anymore because I was suffocating underneath them. Each label told me something that I was: too sensitive, needy, incapable, silly, loud if I wasn't quiet enough, mean if I wasn't nice enough, inappropriate, unladylike, unbecoming, nasty, angry, gullible, naive. I was like a sailor when I cussed, like a virgin when I played innocent, like a slut when I played not so innocent. I was a bad girl and then a good girl. In short, I was a mess.

Unworthy, incompetent, irrational, inferior. Oh, and on top of that I needed to smile more and think and talk less.

No wonder I didn't recognize the woman in the mirror.

When I began my own healing journey, it was this acquisition of sticky notes all over my person that I needed to address first. Otherwise how could I heal if I defined myself by what others – but most importantly the one who had broken my heart – said about me? Though it was an arduous process and not easy by any means, all it really took was my willingness to examine the source of these labels in my head. All of the words that we call ourselves are simply projections of others upon us. If you were told that you're too sensitive, etc., by the one you loved, then it's essential for your recovery that you recognize this label doesn't belong to you. And by the way, there's nothing wrong with being sensitive. The key is that only you are the one who decides what adjective to describe yourself on any given day (and those adjectives will change as you do). Always remember, an abuser has an agenda, and that agenda includes demoralizing a victim to better control them. Hence the use of words. Once you can separate the voice of the one that hurt you and the voice of that girl, however, you'll be able to toss out what's not serving you and recognize the difference immediately when any voice pops up in the future.

Herein lies the beauty of what it is to be truly free. And it's that girl who will help you find this freedom once you decide to not only give her the room to speak but believe what she's telling you. It's a wonderful feeling to be in total control of your emotions and no longer allow others to manipulate you through them. Because it's time you were the author of your own story and put the pen in your own hand. *You and only you are the authority on your experience.* Therefore, you are the only one to say who you are and what you're feeling no matter the day or season. This is so important to remember as you take each step forward in your recovery. Maybe you're feeling extra emotional today, or maybe you're angry. Maybe you feel like raging, or like finding a corner in your house to crawl into and cry. Maybe you're feeling empowered and a little goofy because of it. Maybe you feel like laughing so hard that people will wonder what's wrong with you. Or maybe you're feeling vulnerable and need to reach out to a good friend or trusted family member for a hug or a glass of wine (or three, I'm not judging). The point is, whatever description you feel like owning, it's yours to own. And when you feel like changing the adjective that describes you, change it. No one else has the right tell you who you are, what you want, how you should feel, or what you should do. You are the only one with that power.

***

Now, I want to let you know that while it's true that healing is a lengthy process and requires your full attention and honesty, you're not alone in this. Don't rush your transformation. You know by now that the only way is through, but it's also important for you to know that many an abuse victim has taken this journey and has done so in their own sweet time. Oh, if only it were that simple to just move on and never look back. But that's a fantasy that only happens on television when thirty minutes is enough time to experience the problem, face the problem, and solve the problem before the credits roll. Unless we are blessed with magical powers (I was always so jealous of Samantha on *Bewitched* and her ability to wiggle her nose and make everything as she wanted it), rebuilding a life after abuse is no easy task and takes time and patience. In addition, remember that healing is not a linear process. There are ups and downs and forwards and backs to the point where sometimes you're going to get dizzy. Sometimes it can feel like the rug has been pulled out from under you. Let's think back to that hurricane analogy I spoke about before. Let's say your heart is a house where you've stored everything you love most in the world. Then, without warning, a category 5 hurricane barrels through one night and rips your home from its foundation, the winds sweeping up everything inside of it and tossing it miles away, leaving you breathless and naked in the center of what used to be your life.

According to those people who think they know you and how you should heal, all you have to do is put those magical powers of yours to use, blink, and make everything go back to the way it was, right?

drop f-bomb here

Recovering from any type of abusive relationship takes time, honesty, compassion, love, and many, many hugs for yourself (and maybe some tequila, full-body massages, or nights out salsa dancing). You are rebuilding everything about your life, and that can't happen overnight. As I write these words, I want to wrap my own arms around you and hug you through this because I know what it takes. I've been there. I once stood alone and afraid once the hurricane roared through and destroyed everything I knew. Then I began the process of picking up the pieces, scouring the rubble, and trying to rebuild but not knowing what my new life would even look like since I had spent so many years focused on building the life I already had.

When I look back on my journey of recovery and healing, I see myself after the hurricane slowly but surely building a new house (figuratively speaking) where my children and I could start over again. But remember when I said that healing wasn't linear? Well, once I began the process of rebuilding, there came other storms, even smaller hurricanes, that would blow through and shake me up all over again. When my ex spent the first year hoovering me (named after the Hoover vacuum, it's a narcissist's way of trying to suck you back into the relationship) and I kept falling for his act, I had to take fifty steps back as I dealt with the heartbreak of who he really was all over again. So even though I had built my new house, once in a while a strong wind would come through and take out a tree or a piece of fence; then I'd have to spend the time putting things back together again. Nowadays, and only because we share children who were also victims of his emotional abuse, I still have to deal with some smaller storms that may knock a few shingles off my roof every once in a while. But now I'm equipped to handle the weather no matter what blows my way, so I simply wait until the sun shines again. And once you're fully detached from your pain and past, the sun always shines again.

In addition to recurring storms that will try to interrupt your progress of recovering, nowadays it's also much harder to heal from heartbreak because of the internet. If you're not careful and know how to avoid it, signs of your ex will pop up all over the place and cause you an incredible amount of grief that is capable of pulling you back to Point A if you don't know how to handle it. Let's use that "your heart is a house" analogy again. If a hurricane destroys your home, you're not going to build the exact same home made out of the exact same materials again, right? That would be really stupid and asking for trouble. When you rebuild you want to put in those extra precautions and safety measures so that if a hurricane came again you'd be prepared. During the healing process, it's crucial to take these measures to protect yourself from being dragged back to your past pain and also from making the same mistakes in the future. One of these precautionary measures involves the removal of your ex from your personal space, which includes social media. Tempting as it may be to see what (or who) he's doing, you know very well that's nothing short of masochistic and will get you absolutely nothing but a stomachache.

Social media, but especially Facebook, can be brutal to a soul that needs to heal. Remember those voices I told you about? On Facebook those voices are amped up on crack and once you start listening to them it's really hard to stop. Combine that with the voices in your head and prepare yourself for a lot of frantic sweating and anxiety attacks, which typically occur at two or three in the morning. This is particularly true if you're dealing with a narcissist who is like a vampire and will suck the life out of you at every opportunity. The way they do this is twofold: Either they will post their new life on Facebook and try to make you jealous when you see how happy they are without you (they're really not, they're just trying to make their internal shame for being such a douchebag go away) or they will bombard you with pleas of reuniting and beg you to return with promises of change (FYI: narcissists never change; they only get worse). Another tactic they use is called bait-and-switch. They will lure you back into their midst by love-bombing you like they did in the very beginning; then once you're trapped in their snare, they'll switch back to being cruel and unforgiving. This is a game you can't win, so I strongly suggest you make a vow to not play anymore and then stick to it.

Back in the day (my day), we had the space to get over our exes because once inside the privacy of our own homes we could hide away and nurse our wounds until the day came when we were ready to leave our cocoon and face the light again. Today, however, with the ever-present option of the internet, we have no such privilege. If we're not careful, any healing and recovery we're attempting is immediately thwarted by Facebook tempting us at every level to *just take a peek* at what our ex is up to. What could be the harm, right? After all, you don't want him anymore (or you don't *want* to want him anymore), so how could one little glimpse at what he's up to hurt?

This is *in a Julia Roberts* Pretty Woman *voice* a big mistake. Big. Huge.

Here's why: If you want to get rid of your emotional attachment to your ex and truly move on to the next phase of your life, then you must close all those doors that could potentially lead you into the dangerous territory of *Can you believe him? Well la-dee-freaking-da he sure moved on quickly!* After all you've been through, do you really want to keep feeling this? Of course not, and you deserve so much more. You deserve the space to heal after what you've experienced. So it's time to purge and rid yourself of every single ounce of energy that isn't serving you, which includes an ex who may be determined to still hurt you.

When I left my second husband and our union of sixteen years behind, not even a month had passed, nor had I yet filed for divorce, when I unfriended him on Facebook (the only social media account I had at the time). I somehow knew that I had a lot of healing in front of me and I wouldn't be able to sufficiently move forward if I were constantly dragged back into the pain by posts that reminded me of my heartbreak. After all, I had enough pain to deal with, such as the reality that my ex destroyed our marriage by screwing around with teenage girls less than half his age (don't worry, they were legal, as if that makes it any less disgusting). Once I left him, I didn't want any updates on how he was furthering those relationships. I didn't need to see who was living in the dream home that we had built together for our family. I didn't want to know which adolescent Goldilocks was sleeping in my bed. And I definitely wasn't prepared to see how easily I had been replaced at the age of forty-five with a twenty-something-year-old girl.

Thank you very much, but *no*. I had a lot of healing and recovering to do, along with having a new life to build after my old one was shattered without my consent. I was fortunate in that I was able to leave the small town we lived in and move back to my home state of Arizona, where the sun was waiting for me (still not quite sure how I made it through sixteen Wyoming winters, but that's another story). So after unfriending my ex on Facebook, I also unfollowed every single person I knew in the small town we had lived in so I wouldn't risk seeing random posts popping up that may have included snippets of my ex's shenanigans. At the time, I couldn't even handle seeing a picture of his face since it reminded me of how I had been duped into believing he was a good man and that I was safe in his hands. This is typical for abuse victims. We simply cannot handle even the slightest trigger of the abuse because it could set us back for days, even make us physically ill. I cannot stress enough how the more you crack open that door for your ex to creep in, the more vulnerable you are to interrupt your recovery or even abandon it altogether.

Bottom line: If you're serious about leaving the pain of your abusive ex behind you for good, you need to do some serious cleaning up on your social media accounts, starting with making it seem like he never existed in the first place (at least by Facebook's standards). Unfriend. Unfollow. Block if you have to. And delete all temptation to go backward to a place you know you don't want to be. Then it's time to get on with your healing and using social media to your advantage (there are numerous private groups for narcissistic abuse victims on Facebook, for example) by adjusting your settings on your daily feed to allow only that which will benefit you. Take back control of your social media life by remembering that you and only you have the power to let in or shut out certain people. This is all part of rebuilding that new house of yours that needs to get up to code in case another hurricane hits.

You've got this, my love. You hold all the tools you need in your own hands to not only rebuild that big beautiful heart of yours, but also protect it so no outside enemy could ever get in again. All of your wounds will soon be filled with so much light that you'll have to shield your eyes from the glare. So let's take that next step, shall we?

Love is waiting for you.

WE DON'T RUSH THE CATERPILLAR
healing takes time

"Time is the longest distance between two places."
– Tennessee Williams

What you do *while* you are healing will make the biggest difference in your recovery. Since time is in abundance, there will be moments when you may be tempted to go back to the one who hurt you. Of course, you can lessen your risk by minimizing or blocking anything related to your ex. But considering the vulnerable state you're in, and especially if you don't have anyone you can really talk to or trust with your pain, it's more than likely that temptation will knock on your door in your weakest moments and ask (maybe beg) you to come back. This is one of the biggest mistakes women make since it is a fact that you cannot heal in the same environment that broke your heart. In our suffering we want so badly to believe that "he's changed" or "he really does love me" (both statements I've heard in abundance from women over the years). But here's the truth: If he truly loved you, he wouldn't have hurt you to such a degree in the first place. He wouldn't have disrespected you, lied to you, manipulated you, cheated on you (and make no mistake – abusers know what they're doing and they do it intentionally and with purpose).

If you want to fully escape, recover, and heal, you must get on a one-way road in the direction of *away* from he who caused your pain. This is the only road that will lead you into the light and away from the darkness. Even if you don't know where you're going, as long as it's in the direction of forward you're going to get there. As Rumi said: "If all you can do is crawl, then start crawling." I remember there were months that would go by when, every morning when I woke up, I had zero idea of what was ahead of me or in what direction I was headed. So I didn't focus on that. Instead, I focused on moving through the day with the intent to end it at night having not gone backward in any way. As far as those days spent on the floor in a sobbing mess and unable to get up? I did eventually get up. I did eventually stop crying. And then even if I moved slower than a snail (or my middle son getting ready for school), I still moved. What is time, after all, except what we make of it? I had spent sixteen years of my life loving and planning and hurting and breaking, so I decided right at the beginning of my healing process that time would no longer be the boss of me and I was no longer going to define it like I had in the past with hours and minutes, months and days. Instead, I would define time by the expansion of my heart and the seed of hope I had planted in my soul, which I now cared for and watered every day to some degree or another.

This is your moment of hibernation, reflection, and awakening. You are essentially in a cocoon that is shielding you while you metamorphize into the woman you were always meant to be. Think of it like a birth. A rebirth. Remember, though, birth isn't pretty. When we think of a birth, we tend to think of a new baby. We can picture it in our minds. The new baby is beautiful and perfect and worth all the pain we produced to birth it. But in doing this we're missing a fundamental part of the birthing process, which is anything but pretty. Think of a foal coming out of its mare mother, a chick bursting from an egg, or as in my case, with two of my three kids born by cesareans, well, if you're looking for a beautiful birthing experience, I can tell you that that is definitely *not it* (I still to this day am convinced the doctor shoved my intestines back in the wrong order).

Rebirth is no different. In fact, I would argue that it's even messier and uglier. If you were in an abusive relationship that wasn't physical, you won't have any outside indication of your wounds that would give away your pain, but your poor insides have taken quite a beating. When our hearts are broken and our dreams shattered, when our illusions are smashed and all our previous plans for the future have died a horrible death, there isn't a place within our physical body that doesn't suffer from the consequences. Many victims of narcissistic abuse suffer from anxiety attacks, ill health, and complex PTSD. My own experience included me going from a healthy, physically fit dancer and holistic health coach to a panicked, frail, paranoid mess who stopped going out socially –even trips to the grocery store were fraught with thoughts of *I need to get home* so I could hide.

Whatever your recovery cocoon looks like, the point is that you understand it's a cocoon and there is work to be done in there before emerging. This work you're doing isn't pretty and it doesn't feel good much of the time. You're going to be uncomfortable. You're going to sweat. You're going to feel so squeezed in that you want to break free and go running for the hills. But this is exactly the point. *This is how you know your recovery is working*. This is how you know you're moving forward. There are things that are dying inside of you – dreams, illusions, misconceptions – and that's OK because at the very same time there are things growing, building, and shaping within. Like the cells of your body, every moment of time there are cells dying and cells regenerating. This is forward movement. You don't feel your cells doing this, much like when you're recovering you often don't feel like you're making any headway toward healing, but it's happening nonetheless. Sometimes we just have to put our daily lives on autopilot (or let that girl take the wheel) and put our trust in the process that promises we will come out eventually on the other side. We will emerge out of our cocoon. We will be born again. We will become the butterfly.

One of the things I ask many of the women I work with is to look into the future, not to try and envision where they're going to be at a certain point (because when we're healing we can't see into the next hour let alone the next year) but to ask themselves how they want to *feel*. This especially helps if you're still in the tug-of-war with your heart that is tempting you to go backward to the one who hurt you. Because let's be honest, much of the time we simply feel like crap. This is because we've lived in the darkness for so long that we're unsure if we've still got one foot still stuck in it. In that darkness, where we mistook abuse for love, our thoughts get muddled because we stop seeing the difference between reality and what our abuser created for us to believe was reality. This is why victims of abuse spend so much time in confusion and not knowing which way is up. In order to find clarity and clear the fog, it's a good idea to get in touch with how we used to feel, how we're feeling today, and how we would like to feel in the future.

Ask yourself: How do you want to feel a year from now? Not where you would like to be or see yourself. Tap into those core emotions – ask that girl to help you get there. Do you still want to be feeling heartache all the time? Do you want to be confused and unsure of what you're doing? Do you want to feel emotionally attached to your ex? Do you want to still feel played like you're the puppet and he's the puppet master? Or do you want to feel free from all of those feelings? Even if you're still unsure of where exactly you're headed in this new life of yours, do you at the very least want to feel *less pain* than you do today?

If so, then use that goal as a roadmap to get you there. Write it down on a sticky note (better than having one written for you by someone else, right?) and put it on your bathroom mirror where you can see it every day. When I was hurting the most, I would look into my eyes in the mirror and repeat: *You've got this. You're strong. You're smart. You're beautiful. You've got this.* Many times it was with tears in my eyes after having been dealt another emotional blow by my ex, and yet this verbal act still emboldened me to take a deep breath and keep on rowing no matter how fast the rapids were or even if it felt like I was going upstream most of the time.

Remind yourself of how amazing you are. If you can't remember, ask that girl. She knows it very well. Think back to a time – at whatever age it was – when you knew you were amazing. Remember how it felt to be so empowered and in love with yourself? Remind yourself of that strength that never died within you. It may have hid from you for a while, unable to bear the weight of suffering at the hands of someone you loved, but it was always there.

Have you ever been walking down a sidewalk and see a dandelion pushing up through a crack in the concrete? That's how strong you are. You have the ability to push through anything, to carve canyons out of mountains, to create light where there is only darkness. The place where you find that strength? You're going to take every ounce of energy, love, compassion, and patience that you used to spend on someone else and redirect it toward yourself. You've already given too much, even borrowing against your heart while the one you loved gave nothing in return. Now it's time for you. Do you find yourself feeling sorry for the one who hurt you? That girl will tell you that you need to stop that right here and right now. Absolutely no energy should extend in any direction than your own (and your children if you have any). You've already sacrificed so much. Now is the time to just think of *you*. Trust me, abusers – especially narcissists – will be *just fine, thank you*, so no need for you to worry about how they're doing.

This is the perfect time to fill you in on a little secret about your suffering: *Love didn't hurt you. Someone you loved did.*

This frees you up to still hold on tight to that love you're filled with and just extend it in the direction of the person who deserves to receive it: you.

One way to do this is to surround yourself with beauty and rid your life of anything toxic that threatens to disrupt your recovery process. If you've been involved with a narcissist, you know their ability to convince even your own family members to turn against you. Since narcissists create smear campaigns while you're still very much in the relationship with them, which convinces people you know and even love to somehow believe his narrative of you instead of the truth, remnants of such smear tactics will often follow a victim far past the breakup. When I left my narcissistic husband and the town we lived in, I lost everything, including two of my dearest friends (or those I thought were my dearest friends). They simply couldn't get off the fence and pick a side. And I needed them to pick a side – my side – because they were my closest friends and I needed their friendship. But my ex had already begun a narrative against me that cast me as the perpetrator and him as the victim. Plus, he was incredibly charming and flirtatious, so I stood little chance in trying to win anyone over. Because of that, I needed to remove anyone who was not 100 percent in favor of my well-being and happiness from my immediate space. This included my own father. He chose to side with my abuser and even went out of his way to pursue a friendship while at the same time I cried and begged him to be on my side. When I realized my own dad just couldn't do the right thing, I decided that for the sake of my own emotional survival I needed to remove him from my life.

So when I say surround yourself with beauty, I also mean rid your life of everything that is not offering beauty to you. Whether it's friends or family members or acquaintances, or even a job or house or a place (granted these are more difficult to change, especially in times of crisis), you deserve to be surrounded by only that which benefits and serves you, that enriches instead of takes away, that lights up instead of casts a shadow. This doesn't need to be accomplished with any confrontations or anger or aggression. It's a simple removal of your being from any darkness that threatens to swallow you up.

Then, once you're standing in the full light of your life, use that space to bring in even more beauty. If you can't remember what you used to love in life, that girl does. She helped me when I was at the turning point of figuring out what to do and reminded me of all that I had loved before all that I had lost. Thus I began exploring. I found old loves that I had forgotten about and new ones that I was excited to try. I began meditating and attending a Buddhist temple, which taught me how to go inside myself and find the light to heal all that was hurting me. I created my own yoga practice and spent my mornings (still do) listening to my favorite songs and stretching my limbs in the sun's rays on my bedroom floor while manifesting my visions of the day and celebrating the strength and muscle of my own body, which had in the past always brought me such suffering. Since I had moved back to the beautiful weather of my home state of Arizona, I started hiking. Most of the time I went by myself, but the feeling of pure joy when I reached the top and had my lungs full of fresh air was comparable to nothing I'd ever experienced before. Whenever I was feeling especially down or heavy with thought, I simply hiked it off since there's no room for it at the top. I also started dancing again (my ex and I owned a dance studio, which had been my life for over a decade) and also began venturing out socially to new places, new experiences, new restaurants and movies and local events that I would never have attended in my old life.

During your recovery, rediscover what brings you joy. Nothing is off limits. Do what you always wanted to. Do what people (or your ex) told you that you couldn't. Find your passion again whether it's in the smallest of acts like taking a walk or swimming in a pool. Take all that you're feeling and write it or dance it or paint it or meditate on it. Love yourself up to the point where when you look in the mirror a smile automatically lights up your face.

You deserve it. You deserve beauty in your life. You deserve kindness, grace, and tenderness. It's time for you to step fully into the light and claim your space in it so that everyone knows you're no longer interested in going back to the darkness.

You may be a big girl now, but all those little girl dreams you had are still within your reach. That girl has been loving you over all these years, waiting patiently for you to finally love yourself. There is no better time like the present to start.

FOR THE SAKE OF THE KIDS
the collateral damage of an abusive parent

"A good father does not abuse his children's mother."
– Lundy Bancroft

There is no room in this chapter for excuses, folks. Simply put, there is no such thing as "He abused me but he was a great father." Because when a man demeans, disrespects, lies to, and purposely tries to break the spirit of the mother of his children, he is affectively abusing his children. It's like secondhand smoke. The children may not be the ones putting the cigarette to their mouths and inhaling, but it's still as damaging simply because of their vicinity to the poison.

So, let me repeat for the people in the back: *Good fathers do not abuse*. Period.

99

In addition, when a man abuses the mother of his kids, he is cheating them out of their right to have a healthy and joyful mother. Case in point: I used to be a really great mom. I was on it. Every day. And though motherhood was the toughest thing I'd ever done, I absolutely loved it. I was happy, and that happiness passed on to my children. Then my world grew darker as the years passed, and suddenly I transformed into a mom I didn't recognize. I was depressed, sullen, quiet, angry, and exhausted. Because of the abusive relationship I was in (that I wasn't aware I was in), I felt too depleted to give myself to my kids as I used to do. I faked joy in life until the day when I no longer had the energy or desire to fake it anymore. I became a shell of the mother I used to be, and of course I blamed it all on myself. My husband, naturally, blamed me too. He told me that the reason I was such a mess was because I couldn't handle my own children. He often compared me to his sister, who was an incredible mother, and reminded me of my inability to compete with her all the time. Then he compared me with every other mother in America. They could all do it. Why couldn't I?

At the time (when we had three boys under the age of eleven), I didn't think I was asking for much. I had suffered from postpartum depression after our third child was born, so once in a while on a Sunday (when my husband didn't work) I asked if I could go grocery shopping by myself. And once I asked if he could watch my infant and toddler while I went to get my teeth cleaned. *Figure it out*, he told me, *like every other mother does*. So, I imagined a scenario where I would hold my baby, nurse him if needed, while my right foot hung off the dentist's chair and rocked my toddler in his car seat. This of course never happened, which proved my inherent belief that I couldn't hack it as a mother since I didn't go to the dentist until my kids were in daycare two years later.

By the time I ended up leaving my marriage, I felt like I couldn't cut it not only as a mom but also as a human being, since my whole life had revolved around my children and my desire to do what was right by them. Once I began my healing journey, I soon realized that the cocoon I was wrapping myself up in also needed to be big enough for my kids to huddle up in with me. I needed to create a safe place for all four of us because the storms hadn't stopped once I filed for divorce. In fact, they got much worse.

The challenges that come with sharing children with a narcissist, which is a whole different ballgame (as is the divorce process, but that's another book entirely), is the topic I am asked about more than any other from women who are trying to heal after narcissistic abuse.

If this is you, the first and most important thing for you to know is that *there is no such thing as co-parenting with a Narcissist.* It's impossible for the sole reason that a narcissist will do whatever it takes to ruin you, punish you, and hurt you (especially if you are the one who left him), no matter what or who gets in the way. Children become collateral damage when a narcissist rages through like a wildfire and leaves a charred wake behind. All of the tactics that a narcissist used on you, such as ignoring boundaries, lying, and launching smear campaigns against you, will spill over onto your children once you've separated. Thus, the first thing you need to do is make sure that all those illusions and preconceptions about the one you used to love are no longer taking up space in your heart and soul. For your children's sake, you need to expect the worst and never for one moment let your guard down as to what your ex may be capable of. *Because narcissists are capable of anything.* There are entire books on this subject, and all you have to do is google "parallel parenting with a narcissist" and you'll have reading material for years.

My own greatest heartbreak came when I watched each of my three boys suffer to one degree or another at the hands of their father. Though when my firstborn was young my husband took out his rage on him verbally, by the time he entered high school he was virtually ignored. That is, until the time of our divorce, when my husband claimed he wasn't even his son because he wanted to escape having any financial responsibility (he had legally adopted my oldest and given him his last name). My middle son bore the brunt of his father's anger and when he was still a little boy became the scapegoat, while our youngest became his father's favorite and is still spoiled and given whatever it is he wants (which has made my relationship with my youngest son strained, to say the least, since I dare say *No* to him once in a while). Suffice it to say the trauma each of my sons experienced has left them with wounds that are still tender and healing. This is due to a narcissist's inability to put anyone above their own needs. They are completely and utterly self-serving and thus have little to no care if their own children get hurt in the process.

Narcissists are especially vindictive when it is you who has left them. I remember the day like it was yesterday when my husband told me that I would be sorry I ever left him. I knew then I was in for it because he was a punisher and always had been. During the actual divorce process was when I suffered the most because I had to not only endure his punishments (such as lying and cheating throughout the divorce so he could come out better off and leave me with as little as possible) but also watch my children cry at his indifference and anger and all-around inability to be a loving father to kids who needed one during this difficult time. He lied to our children about me constantly. He manipulated them, especially our youngest who was his "golden child" and adored him, to the point where I would often have to take them aside and assure them that everything was going to be OK, that I would never lie to them, and if they ever had a question they could ask and I would always tell them the truth. But my ex was merciless. When I told my youngest son his father and I were getting a divorce, I begged my ex to not introduce his young girlfriend right away because our son was struggling and was taking it very hard. But my ex didn't care. The girlfriend was already living in our home and according to him she was "really good with children." (Given she was the age of our oldest child, how could I argue?) The bottom line was that my ex put his own needs and desires over our son's. It didn't end well, as my youngest ended up begging me to take him home on that first visit. And he wasn't the only one hurting. My oldest son was constantly worried about me during our divorce, while my middle son would cry himself to sleep at night and often go into rages against his father. My youngest – who began sleeping with me in my bed – continued to suffer silently, sometimes becoming so anxious that he'd throw up in the middle of the night and not remember he had done so the next morning.

***

If you share children with a narcissist, you have your own horror stories, I know. And I know the pain you've felt as you stand by helplessly, unable to do anything about it. I'm here to get not only you but also your children through this recovery since they are going to be only as successful as you are. And you will all get through it. How it turns out or what it looks like may not be your dream come true for your kids, because unfortunately narcissists wield such power that oftentimes children are helpless to resist (such as a child being drawn into the web of a narcissistic parent and turning on you, or one growing up and becoming a narcissist themselves). Abuse punishes everyone involved and creates lifelong scars. I'm here to help you get through this as best you can and do everything in your power to help your children in the best way possible.

You will be much better equipped against a narcissistic parent if you have no illusions about what they're capable of. The trouble I got into when I first left my ex was that I still believed he would never do anything on purpose to hurt his own children. In the beginning, I would still attempt to forge a relationship between my kids and their father. I would still act as the "in between" as I did when they were little and I'd have to mediate where it was necessary. Like many other women do with the men they love, I believed I could make him be a better father. Because of that, my kids paid the price. What I learned is that when I tried to play referee and make everyone happy, I was essentially telling my kids that I wasn't 100 percent on their side and thus invalidated the pain they were feeling because of their father. A psychologist who was an expert on narcissistic personality disorder and who had initially diagnosed my ex told me, "You must stop mediating and start being wholly on the side of your children. Listen to them. Believe them. Stand up for them. You are all they have." From that moment on, I refused to ever be in the middle again. And I then spent every waking minute reminding my kids that I was there for them and only them and would forever be on their side.

Since you will never know the full extent of what a narcissist is telling your kids, what he's lying about behind your back, or what your kids are thinking about it all, the one thing you can make sure you do is to provide a safe and loving space for your children to be in and make sure they know it is a safe and loving space. Your son or daughter may tell you a little bit or a lot or nothing at all about what's being said by their father. They may tell you a little bit or a lot or nothing at all about how they're feeling about. It's not your job to pull that information out of them because the only way to do that would be through pressure and placing them in an uncomfortable position of "Mom vs. Dad." I know it's tempting to try and find out *What did he say about me?* but you're going to be the bigger person in all of this because you love your kids that much. What you'll do instead is make sure that they know – and keep telling them – that they can come to you for anything, that you are their safe place, that you will never lie to them, or that there are things you may not be able to tell them because it's an adult matter but if that's the case, you'll be clear on the reason you're doing it.

When you're with your friends and people who love you and care about you, then let your feelings fly and call your ex whatever name you want, or if no one is around and little ears aren't listening then go for it. I can't begin to tell you how inventive I used to get when I would go on a rant and think up the worst names possible to call my ex, to the point where I would end up laughing at myself for my creativity (I cannot provide an accurate example here, however, because the amount of swear words would alert the censor police and this book would never make it into print).

Thinking about it, however, still brings a smile to my face.

No better time than now to tell you this, but you need to stop *all* judgment for yourself as you walk this line, OK? Remember, feel what you need to feel. Cuss what you need to cuss. Scream what you need to scream. And then get back to the business of being the great mother you are to your children who need you desperately to get through this.

Now, there is a possibility that your children may ask you questions about their father. This can be tricky because you always want to make sure that your own feelings (anger, bitterness, revenge, sadness) do not distort the answer. Again, if you fall back on simply being your kids' safe place, you will only talk to them about aspects that will in some way help them and not hurt them. This is why it is not your job to tell them who their father is. I know it's incredibly tempting to do just that, and I drew blood when I bit my tongue on more than one occasion. Especially if you're at that point in your journey where you're learning all about narcissists and their behavior patterns, plus your own experience at the hands of one, it's enticing to want to share your knowledge with your kids.

Don't.

Here's what I've learned through watching my young boys grow up into big boys and what helped them the most: I allowed my sons to figure out their father all on their own. I didn't tell them who he was, nor did I badmouth him (I did all the badmouthing in private … my besties and my cat got earfuls). This, however, didn't mean I allowed their father to continue his abuse and not do anything about it. I was setting an example for my children, after all, so when there came a point that their father acted in a way that was inappropriate or abusive, I stood up for myself so that my boys could see that this type of behavior was unacceptable. I told the truth so my boys could figure out on their own who was doing the lying. I demonstrated strength so my boys could figure out what weakness in a man looked like. I enforced my boundaries and showed them that there was no room in my world for a man who tries to cross those boundaries. As a woman, I presented a sound sense of self-worth for my boys so that when they grew up, they would know a strong woman is someone not to be feared or avoided or controlled, but loved and respected and admired. And I modeled love, above all, not abuse disguised as love, because I knew that someday my boys would fall in love and create partnerships that I hoped would be built on mutual respect and esteem.

I wish I could tell you that everything by the time of this writing was perfect and all my boys have arrived unscathed on the other side. But the reality is that we are all still dealing with the effects of narcissistic abuse to one degree or another. I will tell you that because I followed a path of taking the higher road, telling the truth, and putting my children's needs above my own whenever dealing with their father, it has made all the difference in how far they've each come. The short run was definitely the hardest. In the beginning, when the chaos really started at the onset of the divorce process, there were days when I didn't believe we'd make it through. But in the long run, the truth always wins. Even if there are consequences and our lives with our children don't end up the way we had hoped, the truth of who you are and who the narcissist is eventually unfolds. It may not be evident to everyone. You may experience loss on many fronts (I went for years not knowing what a "win" even felt like, mainly because the court systems don't care at all if your children are hurting unless they have bruises and broken bones to prove it), but your commitment to the truth is going to be what saves your life. Because you will know that you did everything you could for your kids. You will know you were the best mother you could be and had no responsibility for things out of your control, such as the actions of a narcissistic parent.

And remember that puzzle you're putting together? By keeping your children safe and cozy with you in that cocoon, you're that much closer to completing it. It's through your effort that your family will emerge together as one.

YOU'RE STILL THAT GIRL
and you've got this

"I remember her, the girl within, the girl who ran through those sprinklers, who jumped those fences, who climbed those walls without a second thought to slow her down. That's the girl who I've gotten to know again. She is fun, fierce, and as fabulous as can be."
– Suzanna Quintana

Your puzzle is almost finished. You are standing on a precipice about to emerge from your cocoon and leave your old life – and all the pain and suffering that came with it – behind you for good. You are the dandelion bursting through the concrete and with the help of that girl you are turning your wounds into strength. Love is your superpower and it's time to start filling up that heart of yours until you're bursting with it.

That girl has been right next to you this entire journey and is your biggest fan. She won't let you down now or ever so it's important to make a vow to never again shut her away in exchange for anyone who might walk into your life in the future and ask that you become anything you know you're not. You've got some serious growth game going on! No one is worth sacrificing all of the work you've done thus far to get here. No more being nice when you don't want to. No more watering yourself down so someone else can bloom. No more making yourself uncomfortable so someone else can stay comfortable. You don't owe anyone who is violating your boundaries anything. And it's time you rid your life of this self-abusive behavior for good because the world doesn't need another woman in it who concedes, stays quiet, accepts, puts up with, or allows the abuse of someone else who is disguising it within a package of love. Love will never ask you to sacrifice your self-worth, your dignity, or that girl within who can spot crazy coming from a mile away.

The heaviest obstacle to overcome for a victim of abuse is to recognize her worth in the world, since she has had it annihilated by someone she loved and trusted. In order to put the last pieces of the puzzle together, it's important to retrain your brain and get you back to believing the truth of how valuable you really are. Remember, the one who hurt you did so on purpose – there exists no abuser on the planet who doesn't know what they're doing. Use this as a reminder every time you start going down that rabbit hole of doubt and questioning your value. Your journey thus far has essentially at its core been a quest for self-love, that which wraps you in a big hug and whispers from the very essence of your being, *I'll take care of you*. This is what emotional strength and wisdom look like. And you've had it all along. It was merely buried under all that time of trying to survive the cruel attempts of someone you loved to bring you to your knees. And maybe you were brought to your knees, but then look what happened. That entire time you thought you were buried in the darkness, unable to see the light, you had actually been planted. The seed of your magnificence started growing in that bleak and scary place where the sun never shined. None of the pain you suffered in the past was useless for it was helping you get to the place where you are now.

Your heart is a house, remember? You've simply closed up shop for a while as repairs are taking place. These repairs that you're doing are necessary to protect you from a future where the same kind of man with the same kind of intentions to hurt and control you might walk into your life. After all, we repeat what we do not repair. I did it after leaving my first husband when I skydived without a parachute into my second marriage. I hadn't repaired anything and therefore took my same lack of self-esteem and lack of boundaries from one man to another. I also had muted that girl within and thus was flying blind on my quest for love and acceptance. It was no wonder I found myself where I did. Today my life is a well-protected space of beauty where there's simply no room for any abuse to live and breathe. Narcissists no longer even try to breach my space. I not only know my worth, but as I get older, I keep raising the price and adding tax.

This journey doesn't come without its obstacles, however. And you will be presented (and may already have been) with many. Many of the challenges you will face have a foundation based in guilt. Your guilt. You've been convinced for so long now that you are the problem. Then, once you realized that you are worthy and perfect just as you are, you still struggle with how to move forward and cut those emotional ties to the one who hurt you. So, what do you do? You look for help, and in that help, you find the one word that everyone keeps repeating and telling you that your movement forward is impossible without: *forgiveness.*

Ugh. I remember the first time I heard this word as it pertained to my journey of healing. How on earth was I supposed to forgive my abuser? Especially when he was still actively hurting me either through the divorce process, other family members, or our children? I have no problem forgiving someone when they make a mistake or when they own up to their misdeed and accept responsibility for it. But how do you forgive someone who you know is purposely inflicting pain and hardship? When I used to read over and over again that the key to my recovery was to forgive, I was actually retraumatized all over again since it felt like another blow that my ex had gotten away with that I had to suck up and take. In addition, it felt like forgiveness was all of my energy spent on *him*, leaving none for myself. Then of course the guilt set in, and I went back to that narrative on the tape playing in my head that said I was a pretty pathetic human being because of this one major flaw: I could not, would not forgive the man who abused me and my children.

I believed that this would be the greatest challenge I would face on my road to healing – until, that is, I discovered that forgiveness actually had nothing to do with the one who hurt me and everything to do with that girl within whom I had been neglecting, unaware that she was the one I needed to ask for forgiveness from and who I knew would readily give it to me, along with a big hug.

Your healing is dependent on forgiveness of yourself. You must forgive yourself for all the crimes you believe you've committed but were actually never your crimes in the first place. What happened to you was not your fault. There are abusers and there are victims of those abusers. There are not two sides to your story. It may take two to tango but abuse isn't a dance where two people are enjoying themselves. It's not a he-said-she-said game where both people are at fault and need to take responsibility. Therefore, the only person you need to forgive right now is *you*.

Think of all the guilt and shame you've carried and start there. What are you mad at yourself for? Did you stay too long? Do you feel stupid? Do you feel weak that you put up with it? Looking back, make a list of every single thing that you wish you would or would not have done while in the abuse. Then think of everything you wish you could change about right after it was over and since then. *This* is what you need to forgive yourself for.

Because you're not to blame for what happened to you.

You do not bear the responsibility of someone else who hurt you.

It is because of nothing you've done that prompted someone else to abuse you.

You are not deficient in any way and did not deserve to be abused.

There is nothing wrong with you.

You do not have to change who you are to deserve real love and respect from others.

You are worthy as you were yesterday, as you are today, and as you will be tomorrow.

Forgiveness is the solitary act of looking in the mirror and letting yourself go. In order to fully move on and heal after an abusive relationship, you must forgive yourself for everything you believed you did wrong. It's so easy for us to look back and judge ourselves for things we should have done. But that's not fair. At the time, we didn't know any better. This is why I hear so often from women (and said it myself more than a few times) that when we finally figure out what happened to us, we realize we somehow knew to some extent all along, but we didn't want to know. Not because we're weak. Not because we're stupid or pathetic or doormats, but because we did the only thing we knew how to do at the time, which was try to make it from sunup until sundown without any more additional pain. Besides, when people ask that awful question that I hate so much – *Why didn't you just leave?* – then guess what? What if you *had* left right away? At point A of the abuse? Then you know what those same people would ask you? *Why'd you bail so quickly? Love is hard work. Why did you quit?*

Seriously, you cannot win this game. Why even play? Who else matters anyway besides you and your children (if you have any)? So cut yourself a break for what you did or didn't do in your reaction to the abusive relationship you were in. You simply were not yourself, my love. That girl had been silenced and so you had no North Star to help direct you to the light. You had invested everything you had into someone who tricked you. How were you to know you were being tricked? Let that judgment go. You're not in the witness stand anymore. No one is persecuting you except yourself. It's time for you to forgive. You'll never forget, of course. But in order to emerge out of that cocoon, you need the power of forgiveness to help you build your wings so that once you're ready you'll be able to fly without the weight of your own condemnation to ever weigh you down again.

***

Other challenges you will face on your road to full healing and recovery involve temptations to return to your way of thinking that got you into an abusive relationship in the first place. Again, it's not your fault that someone you loved turned on you and became abusive. But it is important for you to recognize how he even got past step one with you so that you won't repeat these mistakes in the future. This isn't easy, especially for those of us who have been in abusive relationships for extensive lengths of time. If something took twenty years to break you down, then certainly it's going to take a good chunk of time to put those pieces of the puzzle back together. It's easy peasy to get sucked back into old thought patterns that bombard you with messages of *You suck, this is all your fault, who do you think you are!* I'll say it again: this is where that girl can save you. Just ask her whose voice is in your head, and then listen to her when she tells you what to do about it. As of this writing, I've been out of my abusive marriage for five years now, and I still hear his voice in my head every so often. Nowadays, I'm pretty dang good at recognizing it right away though, which is why my dog may hear me once in a while say *Oh piss off* to the empty room.

Healing and recovering from an abusive relationship is not much different than a person who has been in an accident learning how to walk, talk, and maneuver through the day all over again. Trauma has a way of permanently changing us. This is why the act of grieving our old life and our old self is so important. That said, it doesn't mean we can't be changed for the better. Yes, what happened was awful and we wouldn't wish it on our worst enemy. But now that you're in control again you have the capabilities to use what you have learned from your experience and create a life that you have always been meant to live and that you deserve. Will there be setbacks and challenges and obstacles in your way? Absolutely. But despite how you were in the past, today you are strong enough and wise enough to meet those oppositions head on. In the past, your heart was hungry, starving in fact, which is why you ate lies. The key is to remember that that was then and this is now. If your heart is hungry, feed yourself. Let that girl in to love the heck out of you.

Take your time in getting to know yourself again and nurse your wounds, and along the way make sure to ditch any and all blame and shame you're used to carrying and exchange it for compassion, patience, and true love for your beautiful self. It doesn't matter how long it took you to get here. The point is you're here and the world is a better place because you're in it.

Welcome back.

SURVIVING EMOTIONAL ABUSE

"Loving you was like going to war;
I never came back the same."
– Warsan Shire

B eing in an emotionally abusive relationship feels like being sucker-punched, then looking around for the one you love to help you up but discovering that he was the one who made you hit the ground in the first place. It's a relationship of surprises, trick doors, and funhouse mirrors in a circus we don't remember buying a ticket to but then waking up inside of one day and realizing the one we love is the ringmaster.

I've learned that emotional abuse is like a cancer. It's invisible to the naked eye, and it uses that invisibility to its advantage as it poisons a person's body, soul, and mind. Which means that recovering from emotional abuse requires no less time and energy and self-love to rid the body, soul, and mind of such poison.

I've learned that the pain does eventually secede, the tears do eventually stop falling, the fist squeezing my heart until I'm brought to my knees does eventually loosen its grip until finally letting go.

I've learned that it's OK to let go of the illusions that all people are essentially good. The fact is, most people are essentially good and have no ability to intentionally cause intense pain and suffering to another, especially ones they love. But not all people. Not all people.

I've learned that many of the people in my circles of the past – friends, acquaintances, even certain family members – were more comfortable when I stayed silent in my suffering. Somehow my story shed light on a darkness they didn't want to admit existed. Because of that, I've learned how to let those people go and grant them the space to stay in the past, since it would be unhealthy for me (and, frankly, a waste of my time) to use my precious energy or strength to try to pull them to my side. The fact is, some people will simply keep their position on the fence. I've learned that it's in my best interest to leave them there.

I've learned that PTSD is not just for soldiers, that a battlefield can sometimes look exactly like a human heart, and that while wounds eventually close and heal, scars remain forever. But I've also learned that eventually these scars will be void of any emotional attachment, and that where I once felt shame for possessing them, I am now filled with love for myself since they serve as a reminder of the beauty in me that survived.

I've learned that I am much stronger than I originally believed. There was a point when I existed in the darkness when I would pray for the ability to behave like him – to turn a switch and become cold and unfeeling, to tower over him while he cried and begged for release, to respond heartlessly in reaction to his feelings. I wanted so badly to *give him a taste of his own medicine*. When I was unable to act this way, I realized who the real weak one was and how there is no strength required for a coward to hide behind a mask of cruelty.

I've learned that there is no right answer, no this or that way to recover and heal from the trauma of abuse. There is only movement forward, putting one foot in front of the other, even when we're overwhelmed by the temptation to crawl into a corner and hide out for good.

I've learned that it was in these moments of my intense pain and suffering during the healing process when my heart was doing its hardest work. All I had to do was lean into the pain, feel it, and then move on. It came down to a process that was exceedingly simple at its core: the process of identifying the darkness I was suffocating within, identifying the light in my future that waited for me even though I yet couldn't feel its glow, and then consciously creating movement, no matter how small, to get me there.

Finally, I've learned that we who have experienced abuse are all on the same road, with some of us farther ahead and in a position to throw life preservers to those who have just begun their journey of recovery and who still suffer in the darkness. The stories of those who have survived before us are that which will pull us out of our isolation, since the first thing any victim must recognize is that she is not alone.

This is my hope for you. That my story will serve as an impetus for you to take those initial baby steps away from what's causing you to suffer so that you can live the life you truly deserve. And make no mistake about it: You do deserve it. And that girl knows full well you do. So honor the pain, face the darkness, stand up for yourself, and love yourself through the trauma before pulling yourself with all your might out of that cocoon and into the wide-open sky of your new life where you can spread your wings and fly.

And then, in love, you will rise.

ACKNOWLEDGEMENTS

We who are victims of any kind of abuse are no different from Dorothy in *The Wizard of Oz* as we search for a better life and an end to our pain somewhere over the rainbow while battling flying monkeys and wicked witches, not knowing that the power was in our hands all along. We only needed that special goddess – or goddesses – to point it out.

So to all of you goddesses who came before me on this journey of healing and recovery, those of you who raised your voices and shared your stories that helped me along this yellow brick road, thank you for saving my life. While I was pulling myself out of the darkness and trying to claim my space in the light, I couldn't have made it without the constant support and love from all of you who encouraged me to keep speaking up even when my voice was shaking. I will be forever grateful for all the beautiful women who have come into my life and shown me what it is to be brave, fierce, and how to not hide from the storm but instead adjust my sails. I am one lucky girl to be a part of such an amazing Sisterhood of Survivors.

To all of my high school peeps: I disappeared there for a while, but I'm back and I want to thank you for reminding me of the girl I used to be before being swallowed in the darkness. Thank you for reaching out to me and letting me know that you still have my back after all these years and that I still matter and have as much right as anyone else to take up space on this planet. By getting in touch with the girl I used to be, who was feisty, fun, and a bit of a rabble-rouser in all the right ways, I've been able to recover in a way I never thought possible. CHS Class of '86 still rocks!

To all of my new Facebook friends: I've never met you in person and yet that doesn't lessen how much I value your friendship. I'm in awe of the fearless warriors you all are, and your example has helped me rise above and find my place in the light with enough armor to protect myself for the rest of my days. Thank you for your beauty and warmth and continued bravery to share your stories that made me realize I wasn't alone. I would not be in the place I am today without you. You threw me a life preserver when I needed it, and now I finally have the strength to throw it to the next woman still lost in the pain of an abusive relationship.

To all the good guys: Every day three women are murdered by a man. Eighty-five percent of domestic violence victims are women. In the United States, a woman is beaten every nine seconds. And these statistics don't even include the millions of women who are emotionally, psychologically, and financially abused. So, yeah, it's not exactly a friendly world for women to exist in. But it would be that much worse without you, the men who value women, who honor and lift up and respect the women in your lives. As an abuse survivor, I am not jaded by men in any way whatsoever. In fact, just the opposite. I am grateful for all the good guys, the nice guys, the guys who are loving husbands and fathers and brothers and sons and partners and who cry along with us at the violence or trauma we suffer. I do not hate all men simply because of one man. I know that all men are not abusers just like all women are not victims of abuse. So I want to tell you how grateful I am for your example and your light and for welcoming me back into the world. I may be late to the party, but dang it feels good to finally arrive.

And to all of you still in the darkness, still suffering and broken under the weight of pain at the hands of someone you love: I see you. I believe you. And if you ever wonder like I used to do whether there was a woman out there like you who knew your story and felt your pain, I'm here. And you're not alone.

The team at The Author Incubator has also asked me to acknowledge the Morgan James Publishing Team: David Hancock, CEO & Founder; my Author Relations Manager, Gayle West; and special thanks to Jim Howard, Bethany Marshall, and Nickcole Watkins.

THANK YOU

Thank you for reading my book and allowing me to guide you along your healing journey. Recovering after emotional abuse, but specifically abuse at the hands of a Narcissist, is no easy road to take. Give yourself a hand for making it this far and taking the necessary steps toward the life that you've always dreamed of and that you deserve. One of the crucial parts of healing is in the recognition that we are not alone, and that someone who's "been there" understands our pain and suffering. We're in this together and I'm on the same journey as you, just a bit further ahead. From this vantage point, I can offer my experience and insight to you. If you would like to work with me and need help putting the strategies I discuss in the book into action, I invite you to schedule a complimentary strategy session with me at www.suzannaquintana.com You can also find me on Facebook at www.facebook.com/suzannaquintana

I'm here for you and you're not alone!

– Suzanna Quintana

ABOUT THE AUTHOR

Suzanna Quintana is a writer, abuse survivor, feminist, divine rebel, and single mom of three sons. Along with being a former professional ballroom and Latin dancer, teacher, and choreographer, she is also a board-certified holistic health coach. Suzanna holds a B.A. in History and will graduate with her second B.A. in Women and Gender Studies at Arizona State University in December of 2019.

After escaping nearly two decades of abuse at the hands of a diagnosed narcissist, which included her being cyberstalked, victimized, and physically followed years after leaving the marriage, Suzanna now helps other women heal and recover after abusive relationships and writes extensively on her experience in spite of forces from her past that are still to this day trying to silence her.

Her piece, "Understanding the Language of Narcissistic Abuse," was published by *Elephant Journal* in 2015 and immediately went viral all over the world, was shared over a hundred thousand times with over a million views, and Suzanna still receives letters from both women and men who identified with her story and finally realized they were not alone.

Inspired by the strong and courageous women before her who raised their voices against abuse in any form, Suzanna vowed to never be bullied into silence again. She believes in the power of sisterhood and no longer believes in fairy tales, since she's learned the true joy in life is holding the reins and riding her own horse into the sunset.

Follow her story on Facebook and Instagram. Visit her on her website at www.suzannaquintana.com

Printed in the USA
CPSIA information can be obtained
at www.ICGtesting.com
JSHW020939300324
60227JS00002B/27